TYPEFOUNDING IN

AMERICA, 1787–1825

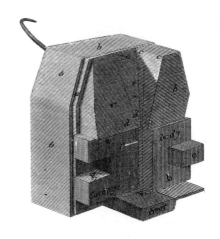

TYPEFOUNDING
IN AMERICA, 1787-1825

Rollo G. Silver

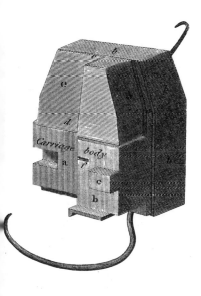

Published for the Bibliographical Society
of the University of Virginia

University Press of Virginia
Charlottesville

TO ALICE

THE purpose of this volume is twofold: to extend
the history of American typefounding beyond the
colonial period and to present a selection from the
specimens of the founders, thereby providing a useful tool for those who wish to know more about the
letter forms cast in America. This basic information, it is hoped, will lead others to more intensive
and specialized studies. Although instances of the
use of specific types in books are noted in the text, a
synthesis of the work of the founders and the books
of the period must await many more identifications.
At times I have been tempted to postpone publication of this study until this synthesis could be prepared; my decision not to do so was abetted by a re-
mark once made by Dr. Clarence S. Brigham, of
blessed memory. "Don't worry about a work not be-

ing complete," he said, "because if it is complete, the next fellow won't have any fun."

The terminal year of 1825 was established because after that date typefounding became mechanized and the "Scotch" faces began to appear. The history of the typefounding industry after the end of typecasting by hand is so transformed and so extensive that many other monographs will be required.

All quotations printed in the text appear without change of spelling and *sic* is omitted after errors.

With much gratitude I acknowledge the help of fellow-librarians and archivists of the staffs of the American Antiquarian Society, the American Philosophical Society, the Columbia University Libraries, the Historical Society of Pennsylvania, the Massachusetts Historical Society, the National Archives, and the New York Public Library (particularly its very efficient Photographic Service). I am especially indebted to Mr. Roland Baughman, Dr. Stephen T. Riley, Dr. Clifford K. Shipton, and Dr. Nicholas B. Wainwright for permission to use and print manuscript material in their custody. Tribute must also be paid to the antiquarian booksellers whose catalogues enabled me to learn of many obscure items. Finally, to the many people who have helped and who are mentioned in the notes, I offer thanks.

ROLLO G. SILVER

January 1, 1964
Boston, Massachusetts

CONTENTS

ILLUSTRATIONS

TYPEFOUNDING IN
AMERICA, 1787–1825

TYPEFOUNDING AS
A PERMANENT INDUSTRY

Although there had been sporadic attempts at typefounding in America since Abel Buell's work in 1769, it was not until the Revolution ended that large-scale typefounding became established. With independence the people of the United States quite naturally began to develop their own industries, thus affording new opportunities to craftsmen across the Atlantic who wanted to emigrate. A British typefounder, for instance, soon became aware that American printers, most of whom used only imported type, would eventually require domestic foundries. Of course the prosperous or better-known founders remained at home, but several of the less important did come to America. The first of these was a Scotsman, John Baine.

When Baine arrived in New York in 1786 or 1787, he had already spent a large part of his long life as a typefounder. His early years remain obscure, but it is known that he was born in St. Andrews about 1713.[1] About 1738 he lived in London where he met a Scotsman from home, Alexander Wilson, a medical student who was alternatively investigating other sciences. Calling at a typefoundry with a friend who wished to make a purchase, Wilson had observed the complicated mode of production and had determined to find a better method. To do so he enlisted the help of his ingenious countryman, Baine. The two men set up a laboratory in partnership, toiling away at their idea, which may possibly have been a form of stereotyping. Eventually they returned to St. Andrews, where they finally relinquished this project and turned to typefounding, devising the equipment themselves. As soon as their foundry opened in 1742 their fortunes began to improve, primarily because, for the first time, printers in Scotland no longer had to depend upon the London or continental founders. After two years in St. Andrews, Wilson and Baine, finding that bulging order books required a location nearer the centers of printing, moved the foundry to Camlachie, a village near Glasgow. The business developed so well that when a representative was needed in Dublin in 1747, the partners drew lots and, as a result, Baine departed

[1] Talbot Baines Reed, *A History of the Old English Letter Foundries*, ed. A. F. Johnson (London, c. 1952), p. 259; Boston *Gazette*, Aug. 30, 1790.

for Dublin, where he managed that branch until the partnership was dissolved in 1749.[2]

Wilson thrived, but Baine's activities immediately thereafter are unknown. Mores implies that he went to London; Bushnell declares that Baine "appears to have remained in Ireland for a considerable period"; Bigmore and Wyman, on the other hand, assert that he settled in Edinburgh.[3] This problem of tracing Baine is further complicated by the fact that his grandson bore the same name. Thus one cannot be certain about the "John Bayne" who was admitted to the Company and Society of Journeymen Printers in Edinburgh on June 24, 1757, or the "John Bain" who printed there about 1760.[4] Nevertheless, two bits of evidence explain that by the middle of the 1760s Baine was casting type in Edinburgh: Alden's discovery of the use of Baine type in America early in 1767 and the Baine type specimen of 1768, now at the St. Bride Foundation.[5]

[2] Reed, *History*, pp. 259–60.

[3] Edward Rowe Mores, *A Dissertation upon English Typographical Founders and Founderies*, ed. Harry Carter and Christopher Ricks (London, 1961), pp. 80–81; George H. Bushnell, "Scottish Printers, Booksellers and Bookbinders," *A Dictionary of the Printers and Booksellers Who Were at Work in England Scotland and Ireland from 1726 to 1775*, ed. H. R. Plomer et al. (Oxford, 1932 [for 1930]), p. 371; E. C. Bigmore and C. W. H. Wyman, *A Bibliography of Printing* (London, 1884–86), III, 87.

[4] *Articles of Agreement by the Journeymen Printers of Edinburgh* (Edinburgh, 1758), p. 18; Bushnell, "Scottish Printers," p. 280. "John Bain" whose widow remarried in 1770 may have been the son of the elder Baine.

[5] John Alden, "Scotch Type in Eighteenth-Century America," *SB*, III (1950–51), 271; Saint Bride Founda-

In the next two decades, the Edinburgh directories, from 1773 to 1786, list John Bain as a typefounder in Calton. About this time his grandson probably joined the firm which, in Edinburgh in 1787, issued *A Specimen of Printing Types, By John Baine & Grandson in Co.*, now at the American Antiquarian Society.

Precisely when and how John Baine and his grandson emigrated is uncertain. Since they were in America the same year in which their Edinburgh specimen appeared, it is possible that the decision to move may have been arrived at rather suddenly. This conjecture is strengthened by the fact that when they left Scotland they had no clear destination. And so the following New York advertisement of August 23, 1787, is important in more than one respect:

Mr. John Baine & Grandson, Letter-Founders, Lately from *Edinburgh*, Having concluded to establish their Type-Foundery at Philadelphia, removed to that city, on the 18th inst. with their founding machinery, leaving, at Mr. David Mitchelson's, corner of Fly-Market and Water-street, the following Founts of Types, For Sale, At the annexed prices, sterling money, viz.

1 Fount of Small Pica,	373 lb. at 1*s*. 2*d*.
1 Ditto Long Primer,	363 lb. at 1*s*. 6*d*.
1 Ditto Brevier,	276 lb. at 2*s*. 6*d*.

Ready Cash or no Purchase.[6]

---

tion, *Catalogue of the Technical Reference Library* (London, 1919), p. 761.
    [6] New York *Journal*, Aug. 23, 1787.

First of all, it implies that John Baine, at least seventy-three years old, arrived in this country without much preliminary investigation into a favorable location. Secondly, it shows that he knew a man named David Mitchelson. One David Mitchelson, as is well known, attempted to establish a type foundry in Boston about 1768.[7] Here, then, is a hint that Mitchelson, a goldsmith and lapidary, may have obtained his casting equipment from Baine, a fellow-Scotsman, but apparently was unable to use it. Thirdly, the advertisement provides the date of the arrival in Philadelphia of John Baine and his grandson.

According to McCulloch, the Baines settled in Philadelphia at the persuasion of William Young, a printer of that city.[8] It was, of course, the most appropriate place, not only surpassing New York in volume of printing but also affording good transportation facilities to other cities and towns. Within a few years the firm was supplying type for some very ambitious publishing projects in addition to conducting what must have been a rather steady business. In the words of Thomas, "They were good workmen, and had full employment."[9] On August 18, 1790, the elder John Baine died, "aged 77."[10]

[7] Lawrence C. Wroth, *Abel Buell of Connecticut* (Middletown, 1958), p. 46.

[8] "William McCulloch's Additions to Thomas's History of Printing," *Proc. Am. Ant. Soc.*, n.s., XXXI (1921), 186; hereinafter cited as *McCulloch*.

[9] Isaiah Thomas, *The History of Printing in America* (2nd ed.; Albany, 1874), I, 31.

[10] Boston *Gazette*, Aug. 30, 1790.

Unfortunately there is no record of a will or administration which might yield definite financial information.[11] His grandson continued the firm though not without at least one effort to dispose of it:

JOHN BAINE, Letter founder, in Philadelphia, intending to decline the business he now follows, offers for sale the whole of the materials which his foundary has been carried on for upwards of sixty years; consisting of between forty and fifty different fixed founts, elegantly cut, with suitable moulds for each; together with punches for the major part of them, which will enable any person who may become a purchaser to strike new setts of matrixes. The terms will be made known, by applying at No. 38, Pine street.

N. B. If a sale is not effected, he means to continue the business to the 1st of May 1794. A person every way capable of conducting the business will be procured.

☞ The different Printers in the United States are requested to insert the above.[12]

The younger Baine carried on for a few more years. His name appears in the Philadelphia directories until 1796 and as late as June 12, 1799, he sold Binny & Ronaldson three hundred dollars worth of tools.[13] While it has been stated that he died at Augusta, Georgia, about the same year, a diligent search of the available records fails to re-

[11] Information in a communication from John E. Walsh, Jr., Register of Wills, Philadelphia, July 5, 1961.
[12] Boston *Gazette*, Feb. 18, 1793.
[13] Alden, *SB*, III, 274.

veal any evidence.[14] Perhaps Bigmore and Wyman were correct when they said that he returned to England.[15]

The American printer who set down the following crisp images of the Baines was William McCulloch. In writing to Isaiah Thomas, he varied the spelling of the surname and touched his craftsman's point of view with acid:

Old Mr. Bayne was an original mechanical genius, and is said to have been the first that communicated any insight into the arcana of type founding to Wilson, of Glasgow. Bayne, in his knowledge of the art, like Fox and Bey, was selftaught. All that he acquired was by his own genius. . . . The son of the old gentleman was a dashing fellow; and I cannot learn that he did any thing at the business. He did not behave well and died prematurely. John Bayne, the grandson, continued the avocation of his grandsire. He and his grandsire, also, cast a good many founts for Joseph James, (afterwards of James & Johnson) a printer of Philadelphia, who soon after gave up business, and retired to Frankford. I possessed, from my father, two of young Bayne's founts, a small Pica and Brevier. The brevier was rather soft in metal, but the fabric, excepting the Italic, good and proportionate. The small pica was a thin faced letter, but excellent metal, with a small portion of silver intermixed; for it was derived from the ruins and rubbish of St. Domingo. Young Bayne, a few years after the death of his grandfather, declined the business. The reason of his relinquishing it, as he himself declared, was, because he could not finish

[14] Information in a letter from Mary Carter Winter of the Richmond County Historical Society, July 9, 1961.
[15] Bigmore and Wyman, *Bibliography*, III, 86.

the type to his satisfaction, owing to his mechanical deficiency in genius and taste. I recollect him well; and he always appeared to me to be much fonder of the table and the toilette than the workshop, Bayne sold a considerable part of his foundry to Francis Bailey: and Binny and Ronaldson purchased a portion, but which has, with them, been long since useless.[16]

Even though McCulloch thought the metal of the pica superior, his own use of the brevier proves that it could not have been very soft; he sent Thomas a copy of his 1815 *Almanac* stating that the brevier in it had been in annual use since about 1795.[17]

No American type specimen of this firm has been recorded if, indeed, one was issued. However, enough items using Baine type have been identified to show that it was approved. In addition to the 1815 *Almanac*, McCulloch told Thomas about two examples of the use of the small pica: "Middelton's Evangelical Biography (12mo. abridged)" and a "History United States first edition."[18] He also noted the *United States Register* for 1794 as an example of the younger Baine's casting.[19] Baine type appeared in William Young's Bible of 1790, in the Isaac Collins Bible of 1791, and, in 1796, the text of Thompson & Small's hot-pressed Bible was set in it.[20] In 1790 the firm's type was used for two very important editions: Mathew Carey's Bible and Thomas Dobson's *Encyclopaedia*. In advertising his Bible, the first American edition of the Douay

[16] *McCulloch*, pp. 186–87.   [17] *Ibid.*, p. 214.
[18] *Ibid.*   [19] *Ibid.*, p. 221.
[20] P. J. Conkwright, "Binny & Ronaldson's First Type," *Printing & Graphic Arts*, I (1953), 27; hereinafter cited as *Conkwright BR*.

version, Carey pointed out that it was printed on type cast expressly for it by the Baines.[21] At the same time, the first of eighteen volumes of the *Encyclopaedia* was issued. For the type of the first ten volumes, one of the most impressive American publications of that time, the publisher turned to the Baines.[22] Thus, within the few years that the elder Baine lived in Philadelphia he had achieved enough significance for the firm to become, as Wroth says, the leading American typefoundry.[23] While Baine type is not remembered for its aesthetic qualities, it did enable the American printer of the period to have readily available good, workmanlike fonts. And one should not forget Alden's finding that twenty years before he arrived in America, John Baine shipped the first Scotch face to be used in the colonies.[24]

Soon after John Baine decided to emigrate, a typefounder on the Continent also began to think of establishing in the New World. The reasons for his desire to remove are known; he, Adam Gerard Mappa, was a displaced person anxious to find a haven. Born at Delft, Holland, on November 25, 1754, he grew up in a middle-class family, entered the Dutch army at an early age, and became a lieutenant in 1771.[25] Nine years later he married,

[21] Lawrence C. Wroth, *The Colonial Printer* (Portland, Me., 1938), p. 110.
[22] *Conkwright BR*, p. 27.
[23] Wroth, *Colonial Printer*, p. 110.
[24] Alden, *SB*, III, 271.
[25] Paul D. Evans, "Adam Gerard Mappa," *DAB*, XII, 265; *American Dictionary of Printing and Bookmaking* (New York, 1894), p. 367.

shortly after which he resigned his commission.[26] While Mappa was still in service, his father purchased a large part of the Amsterdam typefounding firm of Voskens & Clerk at the sale in 1780.[27] Thereupon, Mappa discovered himself to have some talent at typefounding. Apparently he commenced business at Rotterdam; Bigmore & Wyman list two specimens of Voskens & Clerk type which Mappa issued in that city "probably about 1780."[28] Within a few years he moved to Delft in the hope, it has been thought, of associating with a newspaper publisher there.[29] The circumstances of any such arrangement are unknown, but his specimen of oriental characters, 1785, proves that the foundry endeavored to supply a market more extensive than that provided by the local paper.[30] While supervising his business, Mappa, a liberal, true to his zealous conscience, became embroiled in the Patriot movement and led a volunteer regiment in the unsuccessful revolution of 1787. Consequently he was banished from Delft.[31]

His republican friends dispatched him to the Court of Versailles as commissioner to solicit further aid, but this mission was doomed, for France itself was about to endure a revolution.[32]

[26] Evans, *DAB*, XII, 265.
[27] *Ibid.; Am. Dict. Print.*, p. 367; Bigmore and Wyman, *Bibliography*, III, 56.
[28] Bigmore and Wyman, *Bibliography*, II, 21.
[29] *Am. Dict. Print.*, p. 367.
[30] *Ars Typographica*, II (1925), 89.
[31] Helen L. Fairchild (ed.), *Francis Adrian van der Kemp*, 1752–1829 (New York, 1903), p. 143; hereinafter cited as *Van der Kemp*.
[32] *Ibid.*, p. 144.

Mappa lingered there two years, living at St. Omer, the refuge of many other Dutch patriots.[33] At last, discouraged by the upheaval in France, he decided to emigrate to America, accepting the advice of the United States Ambassador, Thomas Jefferson, that he take along typefounding equipment.[34] The foundry which he brought, according to a contemporary letter, contained not only "the Western, but the Oriental languages at the value of at least £3,500 New York currency."[35] On December 1, 1789, Col. Adam Mappa, his wife, and three children arrived at New York after an unusually long voyage of seventy-six days.[36]

At the time of Mappa's arrival New York had never had a typefoundry, and the Philadelphia printers were being supplied by the Baines. Therefore, unlike the Baines, Mappa stayed in New York. By July 16, 1790, his foundry was ready:

A. G. Mappa, No. 107, Queen-Street, Has established his *Type Foundery* in this city, and is ready to fulfil any orders in this line.

Types of every kind—viz.

Roman,	Greek,
Italic,	Samaritan,
Black Letter,	Arabic,
Script,	English Saxon,
German,	Siriac, &c. &c.
Hebrew,	

And decorations to embellish the print, will be

---

[33] *Ibid.*, p. 145.   [34] *Ibid.*, p. 146.   [35] *Ibid.*
[36] Evans, *DAB*, XII, 265; Nina Moore Tiffany and Francis Tiffany, *Harm Jan Huidekoper* (Cambridge, Mass., 1904), p. 35.

attended to with accuracy, and executed on the most reasonable terms.

The respective Printers can also be provided with proper Types, in all the learned languages, so that they may satisfy the wishes of the seminaries of learning established throughout the continent.

The reputation which this Foundery has acquired in Europe, particularly in Holland and England, flatters the proprietor to meet that encouragement and support which he expected from a judicious and discerning nation.

☞ Any JOURNEYMAN acquainted with the business, or Apprentices of the age of 15 years, who are desirous of being employed, and who can produce good characters, will be engaged on equitable terms.[37]

The very extensive assortment of languages presented by Mappa would obviously be more appropriate for a European foundry; in eighteenth-century America the need for books printed in esoteric languages could easily be filled by importation. In fact, Mappa was years ahead of his time. His large stock may have been a compliment to American learning, but it far exceeded the modest requirements of a nascent country.

When the foundry opened, the Mappas looked forward to a comfortable future. To her sister-in-law in August 1790, Mrs. Mappa wrote: "We are well, through God's goodness and fairly well pleased here, we have very good prospects of success with the *Letter-Gietery*, we have a very good and cheerful house very suitable for our business, some good friends, and a contented and thankful heart

[37] New York *Journal*, July 16, 1790.

since we enjoy so many blessings from Heaven above."[38] This pleasant situation, however, soon lapsed so that in January of the following year a letter noted that "all our affairs would go well had we better work people, and a better work-place, but we are obliged to move in May, and, if possible to find a good situation for our affairs outside the city, we shall go, for the pleasure of country life."[39] Unmistakably the shortage of good labor inhibited any progress Mappa could have made. This is dramatically revealed in the story of the 1792 *Laws of the State of New-York.* On July 23, 1791, Thomas Greenleaf announced that

The Editor respectfully informs the patrons of *Greenleaf's Edition* of the Laws of New-York, that in consequence of the favorable reception his proposals met with, he engaged a *new and elegant type* to be made purposely for this work by Mr. Mappa, type-founder, in this city, to be of the same size of the specimen given. The paper on which the work is to be done, is from a manufacture of this state—and thus the materials employed, as well as the matter itself, will be the productions of our own state only.[40]

Mappa, in his attempt to keep up production, evidently had to cast type himself—a task for which he had little training. Mrs. Mappa, writing from New York, September 20, 1791, speaks of his working "early and late, with scarcely time to eat and drink," and using "his unaccustomed hands."[41] Greenleaf, good Protectionist that he was, put up with the de-

---

[38] *Van der Kemp,* pp. 146–47.   [39] *Ibid.,* p. 147.
[40] New York *Journal,* July 23, 1791.
[41] *Van der Kemp,* p. 148.

lays in schedule. Regretting this in his preface to the edition, he also apologizes for the imperfections of the type:

The Types and Paper were manufactured in this State—anxious to give public Satisfaction, and fearing, after the Publication of his Proposals, that the Types therein proposed to print this Work upon would not hold out good to the End, the Editor engaged Mr. Mappa, of this City, an ingenious Type-Founder from Holland, to cast a new Fount for it, which unavoidably delayed the Publication for near two Months. However disagreeable this Delay may have been to the Subscribers (as well as to the Editor, who suffers most by it) it is to be presumed, that the Consideration of giving Encouragement to the Manufactures of our State, will more than compensate. The Types are not so perfectly Regular as those from the London Foundaries, which have been improving for centuries—but, no Cash went to London for them—and our infant Manufactures ought to be encouraged, so that they also may improve.[42]

The lack of craftsmanship in a foundry primarily stocked for Continental business prevented Mappa from capturing his share of the American market. As Isaiah Thomas remarked, "His foundery was designed principally for making Dutch and German types, the casts of which were handsome. Those for roman were but ordinary."[43] If Mappa himself had been a skilled typefounder, he probably would have been able to exploit his large investment. Instead,

[42] Quoted in Henry Lewis Bullen, "A True Protectionist," *Inland Printer*, LXXXVI (1930), 90.
[43] Thomas, *Hist. of Print.*, I, 31.

he found the difficulties insurmountable and soon offered the foundry for sale. When it was sold and to whom cannot now be determined; one statement, undocumented, declares that the foundry was advertised for sale on February 1, 1794.[44] It has also been said that Mappa entered the employment of Binny & Ronaldson.[45] This appears most unlikely because there is evidence that Mappa was living in Olden Barneveld (now Trenton), New York, in the summer of 1795 and Binny & Ronaldson did not commence business until November 1, 1796.[46] At any rate, Binny & Ronaldson probably acquired some, if not all, of Mappa's equipment. According to Theodore L. De Vinne,

The late Mr. W. W. Pasko, who had some correspondence with Philadelphia type founders about Mappa, told me that some of Mappa's types were shown in the Binny & Ronaldson specimens. It is possible that he sold to B. & R. the entire plant of the Mappa foundry. I have a copy of the Mappa specimen book issued by him in Holland. I compared the types in this specimen with those of the early New York type-founders, and am confident that his punches and matrices were not sold or used by any founder of this city.[47]

Although none of Mappa's type can be traced to a New York foundry, some of his matrices did appear in the Binny & Ronaldson collection. Thomas MacKellar, who belonged to a firm descended from Binny & Ronaldson, uncovered evidence in the early

[44] *Van der Kemp*, p. 148.
[46] *Van der Kemp*, p. 151.
[45] *Am. Dict. Print.*, p. 367.
[47] *Ibid.*, p. 212.

records: "The foundry memorandum book of 1822 refers to sixteen sets of matrices as being of foreign production, *i.e.*, from Mappa's Foundry, Rotterdam, whose specimen book is in our possession. These were Greek, Hebrew and German. There were also Persic and other Oriental characters."[48]

Mappa moved to Olden Barneveld after being appointed assistant land agent of the Holland Land Company. Living there on a large farm, he entered community affairs and, in 1797, became agent in charge of the settlement.[49] As a respected leader of a group which included relatives and fellow-exiles, he traveled about the district as a vital force in the settling of that section of the state. Eventually his lack of business acumen led to financial reverses as well as despondency. He died on April 15, 1828, believing that his life had been a failure.[50]

The typefounding ventures of the Baines and Mappa proved that American printers could support a foundry, but only if its production was as skillful as that of the English and Scotch foundries. When this happened in the type of Binny & Ronaldson, the first permanent typefoundry was established in the United States.

Archibald Binny, like Mappa, was a political emigré. Born in Edinburgh in 1762 or 1763, a brewer's son, he did not enter his father's trade but instead became an active typefounder in his home

        [48] "Early Specimen Books and Punch Cutters," *Quadrat*, III (1875), 155.
        [49] Evans, *DAB*, XII, 265.   [50] *Ibid*.

city where, McCulloch says, he cast the type for the standing pocket edition of the Bible.[51] When, about 1795, his advocacy of annual parliaments and universal suffrage was successfully resisted by the government, he decided to take his wife and son to America.[52] Arriving with typefounding equipment valued at $888.80, Binny is said to have experienced some difficulty with the customs office at New York before he finally arrived in Philadelphia.[53]

James Ronaldson, born in 1769, was also a native of Edinburgh, where his father, a baker, officiated at times as burgess and guild brother.[54] The circumstances and date of Ronaldson's move to Philadelphia have not been definitely determined. Bullen states that Binny and Ronaldson were passengers on the same ship; another source declares that Ronaldson arrived in 1794 and opened a "biscuit bakery" which was destroyed by fire in 1796.[55] Nevertheless, on the first of November of that year they entered into partnership as typefounders, with

[51] *Genealogy of the Binney Family in the United States*, coll. C. J. F. Binney (Albany, 1886), p. 222; *McCulloch*, p. 188.

[52] John Finch, *Travels in the United States of America and Canada* (London, 1833), p. 218; *Edinburgh & Leith Directory* (Edinburgh, [1796]), p. 11.

[53] Henry Lewis Bullen, "The Literature of Typography," *Inland Printer*, LII (1914), 709; *Genealogy of the Binney Family*, p. 224.

[54] M. Tait, "James Ronaldson," *The Book of the Old Edinburgh Club*, XXVIII (Edinburgh, 1953), 44–45.

[55] Henry Lewis Bullen, "James Ronaldson's Cemetery at Philadelphia," *Inland Printer*, LXXXIV (1930), 76; Tait, "James Ronaldson," p. 46.

Binny furnishing the skill of typefounding and Ronaldson probably supplying the capital.[56] The house they rented on Cedar Street, at Eleventh, became their foundry and probably also living quarters for one or both partners.[57]

An eagerly awaited study of Binny & Ronaldson is now being prepared by P. J. Conkwright, who has devoted much time to this project. Therefore this study does not propose to attempt a thorough analysis of the firm's work. The comments in these pages will be limited to the most important and illuminating information presently available.

Success came gradually; McCulloch boldly recalls their early struggle:

Binny & Ronaldson encountered many difficulties before they could succeed in obtaining a permanency to their establishment. They offered their type 3 cents a pound cheaper than the importer; but the prejudice against their manufacture was so great, that the European was still generally preferred. Their business acquired the name of an unwholesome one; and many parents would not suffer their children to work at it. However, they worked themselves, every day, early and late, and by not giving out their type till completely finished, began to acquire such credit, that by the end of two years, they could not supply the demand.[58]

By diligently studying account books and by locating examples of use, Conkwright has identified Binny & Ronaldson's first type in four sizes, though

[56] Tait, "James Ronaldson," p. 46; *Conkwright BR*, p. 27.
[57] *Conkwright BR*, p. 27.   [58] *McCulloch*, p. 188.

more were probably available. The pica, long primer, and brevier, he states, "are distinctly old style in character, very similar to those of John Baine, but of better design. The other size, English, is transitional in character, and reflects the new movement then being pioneered by Richard Austin, John Bell, and others."[59] This first type, it must be noted, differed from the better-known Binny & Ronaldson type in the 1812 specimen book. Its use in newspapers, magazines, and books has been cited by Conkwright, who also located the earliest appearance of their type-cast dollar mark—January 2, 1802.[60] According to the account books they charged 33 1/3 cents per pound for English, or over, and pica, and 44 2/3 cents for long primer in 1797. In August of that year they increased the price of long primer 2 cents per pound. The next year the other sizes were also increased by the same amount and the firm received 66 2/3 cents for brevier.[61] Published tabulations of prices for later years appear in various places, but manuscript bills prove that the founders sometimes charged an amount different from the declared price.[62] Account books and bills, therefore, provide the most accurate information.

[59] *Conkwright BR*, pp. 27–28.
[60] P. J. Conkwright, "Binny & Ronaldson's $ Sign," *PaGA*, III (1955), 60.
[61] *Conkwright BR*, p. 29.
[62] One tabulation is in Milton W. Hamilton, *The Country Printer* (New York, 1936), p. 13n. Manuscript bills are in the Mathew Carey Papers at the American Antiquarian Society.

At the turn of the century they found themselves conducting the only typefoundry in the United States. Within a decade they were employing more than thirty men and boys in a lucrative and firmly established business.[63] Extraordinary though they were, they faced the usual vexations common to any manufacturer. Certainly the partners extended large credit; in 1804, for example, Mathew Carey owed them almost seven thousand dollars.[64] Furthermore, they worried about an adequate supply of antimony, the element so necessary for typefounding, which could not be found in the United States, thus making the industry dependent upon importation. When, in 1800, Binny & Ronaldson purchased approximately three tons in London, they insisted that it be shipped in two vessels for greater security.[65] Then, realizing that they would have a considerable duty on the shipment, they petitioned Congress to put antimony on the free list.[66] Although Congress did cooperate by declaring it free of duty in the Tariff Act of 1804, the supply of antimony remained insufficient. Five years later, at the time of an approaching break with Great Britain, Ronaldson voyaged to Europe hoping to purchase antimony in France and Germany. With the help of a letter of introduction from Thomas Jefferson to

[63] *A Specimen of Types Originally Cast in Philadelphia by Binny & Ronaldson* (Bangor, 1949). Broadside.
[64] American Antiquarian Society, Mathew Carey Papers, XIX, 8996.
[65] Rollo G. Silver, "Printers' Lobby: Model 1802," *SB*, III (1950–51), 208.
[66] *Ibid.*, 209.

Quousque tandem abutere, Catilina, patientia nostra? quamdiu nos etiam furor iste tuus eludet?
quem ad finem sese effrenata jactabit audacia? nihilne te nocturnum præsidium palatii, nihil urbis
vigiliæ, nihil timor populi, nihil consensus bonorum omnium, nihil hic munitissimus habendi senatus locus, nihil horum ora vultusque moverunt?
patere tua consilia non sentis? constrictam jam
omnium horum conscientia teneri conjurationem
tuam non vides? quid proxima, quid superiore
ABCDEFGHIJKLMNOPQRSTUVWXY
1234567890

Quousque tandem abutere, Catilina, patientia nos-
tra? quamdiu nos etiam furor iste tuus eludet? quem
ad finem sese effrenata jactabit audacia? nihilne
te nocturnum præsidium palatii, nihil urbis vigiliæ,
nihil timor populi, nihil consensus bonorum omnium,
nihil hic munitissimus habendi senatus locus, nihil
horum ora vultusque moverunt? patere tua consilia
non sentis? constrictam jam omnium horum con-
scientia teneri conjurationem tuam non vides? quid
proxima, quid superiore nocte egeris, ubi fueris,
quos convocaveris, quid consilii ceperis, quem nos-
ABCDEFGHIKLMNOPQRSTUVWXYZ

Plate 1 – Binny & Ronaldson, 1812

Quousque tandem abutere, Catilina, patientia
nostra? quamdiu nos etiam furor iste tuus eludet? quem ad finem sese effrenata jactabit audacia? nihilne te nocturnum præsidium palatii, nihil
urbis vigiliæ, nihil timor populi, nihil consensus
bonorum omnium, nihil hic munitissimus habendi senatus locus, nihil horum ora vultusque
moverunt? patere tua consilia non sentis? constrictam jam omnium horum conscientia teneri
conjurationem tuam non vides? quid proxima,
ABCDEFGHIJKLMNOPQRSTUVWXÆ
1234567890

*Quousque tandem abutere, Catilina, patientia
nostra? quamdiu nos etiam furor iste tuus eludet? quem ad finem sese effrenata jactabit audacia? nihilne te nocturnum præsidium palatii,
nihil urbis vigiliæ, nihil timor populi, nihil consensus bonorum omnium, nihil hic munitissimus
habendi senatus locus, nihil horum ora vultusque
moverunt? patere tua consilia non sentis? constrictam jam omnium horum conscientia teneri,
conjurationem tuam non vides? quid proxima,
quid superiore nocte egeris, ubi fueris, quos con-
ABCDEFGHIJKLMNOPRSTUWYZÆ*

Plate 2 – Binny & Ronaldson, 1812

Pierre S. DuPont, he was able to make the essential contacts and complete his mission.[67]

Meanwhile, the firm continued its progress. In 1806 it secured Benjamin Franklin's typefounding tools and materials from William Duane. According to one report, when Duane offered to *lend* the tools to Binny & Ronaldson, Ronaldson examined them and in delight "at once borrowed a wheelbarrow, and lost no time in personally trundling such as he selected to their foundry, during one of the hottest days in the summer."[68] More equipment arrived in 1810 after their purchase of the foundry of Robert Lothian.[69] The partners even attempted to challenge another industry. One historian of American pottery has stated that they produced yellow and red tea sets in 1808, but this venture evidently floundered.[70]

During this decade, they added a new size of type to their assortment. Equal to two-line brevier and corresponding to the French *gros texte*, it is said to have been first used in Joel Barlow's *Columbiad* (1807).[71] They named the size Columbian, not for the poem, but as they signified in the display in their specimen:

This Letter is a little larger in the face than English, and smaller than Great Primer, and is called Co-

[67] *A Specimen of Types* (Bangor, 1949).
[68] David Bruce, [Jr.], "Type-founding in the United States," *Typographic Messenger*, III (Nov. 1867), 1.
[69] *Am. Dict. Print.*, p. 351.
[70] Edwin Atlee Barber, *The Pottery and Porcelain of the United States* (New York, 1901), p. 111.
[71] *Am. Dict. Print.*, p. 105.

LUMBIAN, in honor of the Country where it was made. It was originally cut for the splendid Bible intended to be published by Delaplaine, Murray, Drape & Co., and is now ready to be cast for such Printers as may order it. If required, it can be cast upon English or even Pica body.[72]

From time to time specimen sheets and specimen books were provided the trade. Some, though probably not the earliest, have survived. The earliest known item, issued in 1809, is a pamphlet displaying 102 metal ornaments, some of which were engraved by Dr. Alexander Anderson. Updike, after remarking that the designs appear largely inspired by French sources, goes on to say:

A feature of the book is its versions of the arms of the United States. Ill-executed mechanically for the most part, from a decorative point of view the collection is respectable and has considerable style. The prices of these cuts run from twenty-five cents to five dollars, and, for the larger cuts in particular, seem high for what was supplied.[73]

The next known item is a specimen of printing types issued in 1812 (Plates 1–3). This contains seven sizes, roman and italic, of a transitional letter, a series of what Morison has called "fat grotesque" style, and some black-letter, Greek, and Hebrew fonts, as well as a showing of ornaments. Of all the faces in this specimen, it is the transitional which has continued in use. Soon after the 1820s it went out of use, but the matrices were preserved and in

[72] "Early Specimen Books," *Quadrat*, III, 156.
[73] Daniel Berkeley Updike, *Printing Types* (2nd ed.; Cambridge, Mass., 1937), II, 154.

ENGLISH BLACK.

And be it further hereby enacted, That the Mayors, Bailiffs, or other head officers of every Town and place corporate, and City within this Commonwealth, Being Justice

PICA BLACK.

And be it further hereby enacted, That the Mayors, Bailiffs, or other head Officers of every Town and place corporate, and City within this Commonwealth, Justice or Justices of peace, shall have the same au=

LONG PRIMER BLACK.

And be it further hereby enacted, That the Mayors Bailiffs or other head Officers of every Town and place corporate, and City within this Commonwealth, being Justice or Justices of Peace, shall have the same authority by virtue of this Act, within the limits and precincts of their Jurisdic-

Plate 3 – Binny & Ronaldson, 1812

Quousque tandem abutere, Catilina, patientia nos
tra? quamdiu nos etiam furor iste tuus eludet? que
m ad finem sese effrenata jactabit audacia? nihilne
te nocturnum præsidium palatii, nihil urbis vigili
æ, nihil timor populi, nihil consensus bonorum o
mnium, nihil hic munitissimus habendi senatus l
ocus, nihil horum ora vultusque moverunt? patere
tua consilia non sentis? constrictam jam omnium
horum conscientia teneri conjurationem tuam no
n vides? quid proxima, quid superiore nocte eger
ABCDEFGHIJKLMNOPQRSTUVWXYZ.

PICA, ON SMALL PICA BODY.

Quousque tandem abutere, Catilina, patientia nostra
? quamdiu nos etiam furor iste tuus eludet? quem ad
finem sese effrenata jactabit audacia? nihilne te noct
urnum præsidium palatii, nihil urbis vigiliæ, nihil ti
mor populi, nihil consensus bonorum omnium, nih
il hic munitissimus habendi senatus locus, nihil hor
um ora vultusque moverunt? patere tua consilia non
sentis? constrictam jam omnium horum conscientia
teneri conjurationem tuam non vides? quid proxim
a, quid superiore nocte egeris, ubi fueris, quos conv
ABCDEFGHIJKLMNOPQRSTUVWXYZ.

SCOTT. $1234567890.   RIPLEY.

PICA, N⁰ 1.

Quousque tandem abutere, Catilina, patientia nostr
a? quamdiu nos etiam furor iste tuus eludet? quem a
d finem sese effrenata jactabit audacia? nihilne te no
cturnum præsidium palatii, nihil urbis vigiliæ, nihil t
imor populi, nihil consensus bonorum omnium, nihil h
ic munitissimus habendi senatus locus, nihil horum o
ra vultusque moverunt? patere tua consilia non sent
is? constrictam jam omnium horum conscientia tene
ri conjurationem tuam non vides? quid proxima, qui
d superiore nocte egeris, ubi fueris, quos convocaver
ABCDEFGHIJKLMNOPQRSTUVWXYZ.

CROGHAN. $1234567890.   GAINES.

Plate 4 – James Ronaldson, 1816

1892 type was cast again and named Oxford. It has recently appeared in another version—Monticello—which is the face used for the text of this volume.

Soon after Binny's retirement, James Ronaldson committed himself to maintain the high standards of the foundry by producing his beautifully printed specimen book of 1816 (Plates 4, 5). In his introduction he paid tribute to his partner, discussed the filiation of sources, and apologized for the fat-faced types:

In August last, my friend, Archibald Binny, retired from the establishment. On laying before you the following specimen, so much the product of his genius and labour, it is due to his character and talents to state, as my humble opinion, that the Letter Foundry owes more of its improvement and simplification to him than to any other individual, since its invention; and the difficulties incident to transferring this business to America, will not be duly appreciated but by bearing in mind that at least seven prior establishments had failed.

In the course of the past thirty-five years, Printing and Letter Founding have very much improved. The new form given to the figures, and discarding the long ſ, has not only benefited the appearance, but removed the perplexity that grew out of confounding ſ and f. Some of these alterations took effect about the same time in America and Europe. In the spirit of improvement, some things were carried beyond propriety: but experience alone could discover what was nearest perfection. To your polite attention, B. & R. were indebted for specimens of the European improvements as fast as they came to the United States. The example of that quarter, having great influence, and, in some cases, strong partialities in its favour, it became necessary for B. & R. to imitate the Europeans, and, in some instances, contrary to their own judgment: examples of this exist in Long Primer No. 2, and Small Pica No. 2. Experience shewed that these were suited only for works of fancy, and led the way to others, in which care has been taken to combine elegance with durability; making the least possible sacrifice of these important properties to each other.[74]

The ranging figures which Ronaldson mentions may have been a simultaneous development. Mc-Culloch wrote to Isaiah Thomas that the "new cut figures, to line together, were cut and cast by them about the same time that those made in London appeared, and without any knowledge of each other's improvement; the American specimens appeared somewhat the first."[75] In this specimen the selection of types and ornaments is, as Updike notes, "considerably increased and bettered."[76] Six years later Ronaldson issued an enlarged edition.

In the prefatory note to the 1822 specimen, James Ronaldson began by pointing to an innovation:

The following Specimen deviates from the custom of English founders: the practice has been, to employ a particular latin sentence; perhaps the object was to enable printers to compare the size of one letter with another, and latin having few ascending and descending letters, shows type to the most ad-

[74] *Specimen of Printing Type* (Philadelphia, 1816), pp. 1–3. Copy in MWA.
[75] *McCulloch*, p. 188. Cf. Updike, *Printing Types*, II, pl. 337a.
[76] Updike, *Printing Types*, II, 155.

Quousque tandem abutere, Catilina, patientia nost
ra? quamdiu nos etiam furor iste tuus eludet? quem
ad finem sese effrenata jactabit audacia? nihilne te
nocturnum præsidium palatii, nihil urbis vigiliæ, n
ihil timor populi, nihil consensus bonorum omniu
m, nihil hic munitissimus habendi senatus locus, n
ihil horum ora vultusque moverunt? patere tua con
silia non sentis? constrictam jam omnium horum c
onscientia teneri conjurationem tuam non vides? q
uid proxima, quid superiore nocte egeris, ubi fuer
is, quos convocaveris, quid consilii ceperis, quem
nostrum ignorare arbitraris? O tempora, o mores!
Senatus hoc intelligit, consul vidit: hic tamen vivi
t. Vivit? immo vero etiam in senatum venit: fit pub
lici consilii particeps: notat et designat oculis ad c
ædem unumquemque nostrum. Nos autem, viri for
tes, satisfacere reipublicæ videmur, si istius furore
m ac tela vitemus. Ad mortem te, Catilina, duci ju

ABCDEFGHIJKLMNOPQRSTUVXYZ.

*Quousque tandem abutere, Catilina, patientia no
stra? quamdiu nos etiam furor iste tuus eludet? q
uem ad finem sese effrenata jactabit audacia? nih
ilne te nocturnum præsidium palatii, nihil urbis v
igiliæ, nihil timor populi, nihil consensus bonoru
m omnium, nihil hic munitissimus habendi senatu
s locus, nihil horum ora vultusque moverunt? pat
ere tua consilia non sentis? constrictam jam omni
um horum conscientia teneri conjurationem tuam
non vides? quid proxima, quid superiore nocte eg
eris, ubi fueris, quos convocaveris, quid consilii c
eperis, quem nostrum ignorare arbitraris? O tem
pora, o mores! Senatus hoc intelligit, consul vidit:
hic tamen vivit. Vivit? immo vero etiam in senatu
m venit: fit publici consilii particeps: notat et des*

ABCDEFGHIJKLMNOPQRSTUVXYZ.
Putnam. $1234567890.   Wayne.

Plate 5 – James Ronaldson, 1816

PICA, Nᵒ· 1.

"The ancients made as unjust wars as the moderns; the difference consisting in the manner of conducting them. The ancients bluntly entered upon their unjust wars, without pretext, preamble, or colour assigned; but the politer moderns first give due notice by manifesto; protest their own innocence, and shew the necessity which, against their will, compels them to arms. Nay, we sometimes beg the divine permission to ravage a country. This appears by the days set apart to implore success to our arms, and the numerous modern declarations of war, wherein the Almighty is called to witness, that force is used unwillingly; and that the contending powers are heartily sorry they are obliged to disturb the public peace."

"*The manners of a people are not to be found in the schools of learning, or the palaces of greatness, where the national character is obscured or obliterated by travel or instruction, by philosophy or vanity; nor is public happiness to be estimated by the assemblies of the gay, or the banquets of the rich. The great mass of nations is neither rich nor gay. They whose aggregate constitutes the people, are found in the streets and the villages; in the shops and farms; and from them, collectively considered, must the measure of general prosperity be taken. As they approach to delicacy, a nation is refined; as their conveniences and comforts are multiplied, a nation, may be denominated wealthy.*"

Quousque tandem abutere, Catilina, patientia no
Quousque tandem abutere, Catilina, patientia nostr
ABCDEFGHIJKLMNOPQRSTUVWXYZ.
ABCDEFGHIJKLMNOPQRSTUVWXYZÆ.
ABCDEFGHIJKLMNOPQRSTUVWXYZ
$1234567890£

Plate 6 – James Ronaldson, 1822

vantage. Only a line of the latin is given in this for the purpose of comparing the size; and the specimen is in the language you will principally employ the type in, trusting its reputation to its own intrinsic merits.[77]

He discounted the attack on his foundry which appeared in a specimen issued by the well-known foundry of David and George Bruce:

A specimen, from a foundry in New York, printed in 1820, has taken particular notice of "The Philadelphia Foundry." Inferences, censures, and self-compliments, are introduced into the preface, in manner and extent which candor and truth should have kept within moderate limits. The publication is incorrect in alledging that the proprietors of the Philadelphia establishment admitted their efforts in improvement to have been unsuccessful. This is not the case; and facts establish the contrary. Compare works of the same class, printed in Europe, with those from the United States, press-work and type— the latter are not inferior to the former; and, except in expensive works, are in most instances better: and the importation of foreign type ceased in proportion as Binny and Ronaldson became known to the printers in the United States. This is plain testimony in favor of the type made at the "Philadelphia foundry," and its reputation, compared with that from Europe.

I have been led into this notice, in defence of the character of Archibald Binny, who we must consider as the father and successful introducer of letter founding into the United States; and whose taste and execution, I believe, are not excelled, and

[77] *Specimen of Printing Type* (Philadelphia, 1822), p. 1. Copy in NNC-Typ.

will long be a standard with us. To him is due the merit of great improvement and much simplification in this business; which, from being of the most difficult nature, his genius has reduced to the reach of ordinary talents. Variations and ornaments may be introduced; these, though displaying taste and gratifying fancy, have doubtful claims to be ranked in the list of improvements. Their principal effect has been to augment the expense, without increasing the quantity of printing; and to impose a serious tax on the printers.[78]

After this counterattack Ronaldson illustrated his argument with an impressive set of specimens, some of which vary in the copies examined (Plates 6–9). They included Saxon, Greek, Hebrew, and German in various sizes of each, more than fifty-five variations of English letters, flowers, and cuts. This was Ronaldson's effective opposition to the Bruces.

The success of the firm proves that Binny & Ronaldson type was of essential value to American printers. That the printers also admired its aesthetic qualities is evinced by its appearance in the *Columbiad* and in Alexander Wilson's *American Ornithology* (1808–14), two of America's handsomest books.[79] Furthermore, it was used by Isaiah Thomas in 1810 for his own *History of Printing in America*.[80] Other appearances of Binny & Ronaldson type are found in T. J. Mathias, *Pursuits of*

[78] *Ibid.*, pp. 1–2.
[79] Lawrence C. Wroth, *Typographic Heritage* (n.p., 1949), p. 45.
[80] *Ibid.*

Plate 7 – James Ronaldson, 1822

PICA, Nᵒ· 2.

Reformation is one of those pieces which must be put at some distance in order to please. Its greatest favourers love it better in the abstract than in the substance. When any old prejudice of their own, or any interest that they value, is touched, they become scrupulous, they become captious, and every man has his separate exception. Some pluck out the black hairs, some the gray; one point must be given up to one; another point must be yielded to another; nothing is suffered to prevail upon its *own principles:* the whole is so frittered down, and disjointed, that scarcely a trace of the original scheme remains! Thus, between the resistance of power, and the unsystematical process of popularity, the undertaker and the undertaking are both exposed, and the poor reformer is hissed off the stage, both by friends and foes. Burke.

National antipathy and prejudice have been cherished by some governments, to secure support from the people in their mischievous wars and ambitious projects; a practice detested by every sensible and generous American. Must we look on other nations as composed of fools or villains, because we have a good opinion of our own wisdom and virtue? Must we be worked into an idea that they are cowards, in order to inspire us with confidence in our own courage? No! Let us have the magnanimity, the justice, and the wisdom to give to all nations their due. Let us dwell on those qualities which exalt, not those that debase them; and let us found our own glory on our own worth; not on their defects.
Russell.

Quousque tandem abutere, Catilina, patientia nos
Quousque tandem abutere, Catilina, patientia nos
ABCDEFGHJKLMNOPQRSTUVWXYZ
ABCDEFGHIJKLMNOPQRSTUVWXYZÆŒ.
$1234567890.
ABCDEFGHIJKLMNOPQRSTUVWXY
ZÆŒÆŒ&.

PICA, Nº· 8.

Speech of Logan, a Mingo Chief, to Lord Dun-
more, Governor of Virginia, 1774.

"I appeal to any white man to say, if ever he
entered Logan's cabin hungry, and he gave him
not meat: if ever he came cold and naked, and he
clothed him not.   During the course of the last
long and bloody war, Logan remained idle in his
cabin, an advocate for peace.   Such was my love
for the whites, that my countrymen pointed as
they passed, and said, 'Logan is the friend of white
men.'   I had even thought to have lived with you,
but for the injuries of one man.   Colonel Cresap,
the last spring, in cold blood, and unprovoked,
*murdered all the relations of Logan, not even
sparing my women and children.   There runs
not a drop of my blood in the veins of any living
creature.   This called on me for revenge.   I have
sought it: I have killed many: I have fully glut-
ted my vengeance: for my country I rejoice at the
beams of peace.   But do not harbour a thought
that mine is the joy of fear.   Logan never felt
fear.   He will not turn on his heel to save his
life.   Who is there to mourn for Logan?—Not
one.*"

Quousque tandem abutere, Catilina, patientia nostr
Quousque tandem abutere, Catilina, patientia nos

ABCDEFGHIJKLMNOPQRSTUVWXYZ.
ABCDEFGHIJKLMNOPQRSTUVWXYZ
$1234567890.

"What conscience dictates to be done,
   Or warns me not to do,
This, teach me more than hell to shun,
   That, more than heaven pursue."

Plate 8 – James Ronaldson, 1822

Literature (1800), T. Moore, *Odes of Anacreon* (1804), R. H. Rose, *Sketches in Verse* (1810), and Adam Seybert, *Statistical Annals* (1818).[81] The pica Hebrew was used in the Horwitz edition of the Hebrew Bible (1814), and some cuts are to be found in *Kurze Beschreibung* (1814).[82]

Binny's talent for producing good type was supplemented by a talent for invention: in 1811 his patent for a type mold, discussed elsewhere in these pages, enabled the plant to increase production. On retirement from the firm in 1815, he sold his half-interest to Ronaldson for sixty-two thousand dollars—another indication of a substantial business.[83] Binny remarried after the death of his first wife, establishing his new household at Portobello, a five-thousand-acre plantation on St. Mary's River, opposite St. Mary's City, Maryland. At Portobello, probably named for the resort near his native city, he employed fifty slaves, operated a weaving factory, milled sulphur and grist, raised tobacco, corn, and wheat. But as he aged and as the demands of the eleven children by his second wife increased, his holdings diminished to a little more than twelve hundred acres.[84] He died April 25, 1838.[85]

Ronaldson continued the business for another eight years, then, in 1823, retired in favor of his younger brother, Richard, who came to Philadel-

---

[81] Darrell Hyder, "Philadelphia Fine Printing 1780–1820," *PaGA*, IX (1961), 80–97.

[82] *Ibid.*, 92, 97.   [83] Bullen, *Inland Printer*, LII, 709.

[84] *Ibid.*   [85] *Genealogy of the Binney Family*, p. 222.

phia after conducting a jewelry firm in Edinburgh.[86] James Ronaldson, a bachelor, was one of Philadelphia's pioneering citizens. He owned and operated the Hillsburgh Mills, which spun and wove cotton, and was president of the Louisville Canal Company. To him can be credited the establishment of the first soup kitchen in Philadelphia in 1805, the founding of a night school, the establishment of the Philadelphia Cemetery, and the first presidency of the Franklin Institute, 1824–41. It is said that he refused a seat in Jackson's cabinet. He died March 29, 1841.[87]

The typefoundry established in 1796 by Binny and Ronaldson continued, under various partnerships and names, until its descendant firm, MacKellar, Smiths & Jordan Company, was absorbed by the American Type Founders Company in 1892. Possessing more constancy and shrewdness than Mappa or the Baines, the two Scotsmen efficiently provided satisfactory type for American printers, thereby placing the industry on a permanent basis.

[86] Tait, "James Ronaldson," p. 47.
[87] Philadelphia *National Gazette*, March 31, 1841; Tait, "James Ronaldson," p. 49.

TABLE for comparing the relative proportions in the depth of line from Great Primer to Pearl:

—●:●—

No 1 Great Primer.

No 2 English.

No 3 Columbian.

No 4 Pica.

No 5 Small Pica.

No 6 Long Primer.

No 7 Bourgeois.

No 8 Brevier.

No 9 Minion.

No 10 Nonpareil.

No 11 Pearl.

No 1.	2.	3.	4.	5.	6.	7.	8.	9.	10.	11.
1	1	1	1	1	1	1	1	1	1	1
2	2	2	2	2	2	2	2	2	2	2
3	3	3	3	3	3	3	3	3	3	3
4	4	4	4	4	4	4	4	4	4	4
5	5	5	5	5	5	5	5	5	5	5
6	6	6	6	6	6	6	6	6	6	6
7	7	7	7	7	7	7	7	7	7	7
8	8	8	8	8	8	8	8	8	8	8
9	9	9	9	9	9	9	9	9	9	9
10	10	10	10	10	10	10	10	10	10	10
11	11	11	11	11	11	11	11	11	11	11
12	12	12	12	12	12	12	12	12	12	12
13	13	13	13	13	13	13	13	13	13	13
14	14	14	14	14	14	14	14	14	14	14
15	15	15	15	15	15	15	15	15	15	15
16	16	16	16	16	16	16	16	16	16	16
17	17	17	17	17	17	17	17	17	17	17
18	18	18	18	18	18	18	18	18	18	18
19	19	19	19	19	19	19	19	19	19	19
20	20	20	20	20	20	20	20	20	20	20
21	21	21	21	21	21	21	21	21	21	21
22	22	22	22	22	22	22	22	22	22	22
23	23	23	23	23	23	23	23	23	23	23
24	24	24	24	24	24	24	24	24	24	24
25	25	25	25	25	25	25	25	25	25	25
26	26	26	26	26	26	26	26	26	26	26
	27	27	27	27	27	27	27	27	27	27
	28	28	28	28	28	28	28	28	28	28
	29	29	29	29	29	29	29	29	29	29
	30	30	30	30	30	30	30	30	30	30
	31	31	31	31	31	31	31	31	31	31
	32	32	32	32	32	32	32	32	32	32
			33	33	33	33	33	33	33	33
			34	34	34	34	34	34	34	34
			35	35	35	35	35	35	35	35
			36	36	36	36	36	36	36	36
			37	37	37	37	37	37	37	37
				38	38	38	38	38	38	38
				39	39	39	39	39	39	39
				40	40	40	40	40	40	40
				41	41	41	41	41	41	41
				42	42	42	42	42	42	42
					43	43	43	43	43	43
					44	44	44	44	44	44
					45	45	45	45	45	45
						46	46	46	46	46
						47	47	47	47	47
						48	48	48	48	48
						49	49	49	49	49
						50	50	50	50	50
						51	51	51	51	51
							52	52	52	52
							53	53	53	53
							54	54	54	54
								55	55	55
								56	56	56
								57	57	57
								58	58	58
								59	59	59
								60	60	60
									61	61
									62	62
									63	63
									64	64
									65	65
									66	66
									67	67
									68	68
									69	69
									70	70
									71	71
									72	72
									73	73
									74	74
									75	75
									76	76
										77
										78
										79
										80
										81
										82
										83
										84
										85
										86
										87
										88
										89
										90
										91
										92

Plate 9 – James Ronaldson, 1822

OME MINOR TYPEFOUNDERS
AND PUNCHCUTTERS

Paradoxical as it may seem, discussion of the minor typefounders of this period begins with a personality to whom that adjective is seldom, if ever, applied—Benjamin Franklin. Yet, on second thought, this is not surprising, for his interest in the industrial arts, selective although not profound, was continuous, and typefounding was very close to his heart. Indeed, it may have been his own ambition to establish a great American foundry that moved him to induce his cherished grandson to enter the trade.

In his youth Franklin cast type, and as an old man at Passy, during his mission to France, he had his own typefoundry as well as a press in his house.[1]

[1] Lawrence C. Wroth, "Benjamin Franklin: The Printer at Work," *Jour. Franklin Inst.*, CCXXXIV (1942), 125–26.

There he printed documents and blank forms plus gay little items; some of his own type he shipped home for sale in America. His friendship with the Fourniers and Didots were of advantage to him in his insatiable craving to be learning something new. Characteristically he strove for efficient operation as well as aesthetic refinements, whether he was experimenting with logotypes, design, or encouraging American printers to buy better type.

While at Passy, Franklin employed a master typefounder to instruct his fifteen-year-old grandson, Benjamin Franklin Bache.[2] For five months young Benjamin steadily worked under his master, so earnestly that, he states in his diary, he had "not paid a single visit during these five months."[3] After this period of intensive training, Franklin arranged to have his grandson work in the foundry of François Ambroise Didot, where, in April 1785, Benjamin cut his first punch.[4] Within a short time, however, the termination of Franklin's mission required Benjamin's return to Passy to help with the packing.

Before leaving France Franklin purchased a foundry from Simon Pierre Fournier and additional punchcutting equipment suggested by young Didot.[5] He also shipped home several sets of ma-

---

[2] Douglas C. McMurtrie, *Benjamin Franklin, Typefounder* (New York, 1925), p. 7.
[3] *Ibid.*   [4] *Ibid.*, p. 8.
[5] Wroth, *Colonial Printer*, p. 112; McMurtrie, *Benjamin Franklin*, p. 8.

trices as well as a sizable amount of type, some, if not all, of which had been cast in his house at Passy. Grandfather and grandson returned to Philadelphia in 1785; the typefounding equipment arrived in March 1786. Resettled at home, Franklin intended to manage the foundry until Benjamin graduated from college.[6] He set up in Franklin Court, Market Street, and proceeded to sell the type he imported. Some business was immediately assured; other sales may have been previously arranged in France.[7] In August 1785, when the Continental Congress requested bids for a new edition of its *Journals*, two printers, with obvious political intent, referred to their use of Franklin's type. Francis Childs wrote, "The subscriber from a Letter received from Doctor Franklin, since his arrival, expects, in the next French packet, a Variety of Types – the Matrixes of which were designed by the Doctor and cast under his direction"; Shepard Kollock submitted documents which had been "printed with a new and elegant Type . . . cast under the immediate supervision of that great Typographer, Doctor Franklin."[8] Unfortunately, Childs did not say more about the designs attributed to Franklin. One group may have been the script type which McMurtrie mentions as

[6] Wroth, *Colonial Printer*, p. 112.
[7] McMurtrie, *Benjamin Franklin*, pp. 8–9; Wroth, *Jour. Franklin Inst.*, CCXXXIV, 126; Edmund P. Dandridge, Jr., "Proposals of Nine Printers for a New Edition of the *Journals of the Continental Congress*, 1785," *SB*, II (1949–50), 195.
[8] Dandridge, *SB*, II, 195.

specially engraved by Fournier, "probably from designs by Franklin."[9]

Although an expert businessman Franklin, probably tired by the pressures of his complex interests
and impatiently marking time until his grandson
could take over, failed to make the foundry thrive.
At the beginning there were deficiencies of sorts;
for instance, Benjamin Bache had to be assigned the
task of cutting new punches.[10] More important was
the lack of acceptance. Isaiah Thomas recalled the
unhappy period: "Although the materials of this
foundery enabled the proprietor to make Greek, Hebrew, Roman, and all other kinds of types in use in
Europe or America, the foundery was but little employed. The implements for making roman and
italic types, especially, would not produce handsome specimens."[11] To improve the design Franklin employed Frederic Geyer (or Geiger), a German
redemptioner, as punchcutter. Originally a mathe-
matical instrument maker, Geyer, Thomas says,
"cut a number of punches, and made great profi-
ciency as a type maker, and in the improvement of
the foundery."[12] McCulloch was also impressed:
"The stamps that Geyer cut exceeded every thing
of the kind that had appeared in America."[13] Geyer
completed the time for his redemption, then left the
foundry for the U.S. Mint, where he worked in
1794.[14] His interest in mechanics led him to experi-

[9] McMurtrie, *Benjamin Franklin*, p. 8.
[10] *Ibid.*, p. 9.   [11] Thomas, *Hist. of Print.*, I, 30.
[12] *Ibid.*   [13] *McCulloch*, p. 185.
[14] Thomas, *Hist. of Print.*, I, 30.

ments in perpetual motion and determination of longitude by lunar observation. "But," McCulloch wrote Thomas, "the perpetual motion turned his brain, and the lunar observations transformed him to a lunatic. Intemperately mad, he was confined in the cells of the Philadelphia alms house."[15]

About 1787, when Benjamin Bache assumed management of the foundry, the situation was irreversible. Three years later he received under his grandfather's will "all the types and printing materials, which I now have in Philadelphia with the complete letter foundery, which, in the whole, I suppose to be worth near one thousand pounds."[16] Bache then operated the foundry as an adjunct to his printing office, for he decidedly preferred to print and publish rather than to manufacture. At some time about 1790 he issued his only known type specimen, which, it must be emphasized, was a specimen of the types available at his printing office (Plate 10). It contained this note:

Besides the foregoing Specimen, the Subscriber has a complete Type-Foundery; Where Printers may, at a short Notice, be furnished with any sized Founts, on reasonable Terms. The Specimen includes a few of the Founts belonging to this Foundery; they are marked with * and may serve to give the Printer an Idea of the whole. A complete Specimen of the Foundery consisting of sixty different Founts, Roman & Italic, three Sizes of Greek, a Pica Hebrew, a great Variety of Flowers, Metal Rules, &c. &c. may be seen at the Printing-Office in Market,

[15] *McCulloch*, p. 186.
[16] McMurtrie, *Benjamin Franklin*, p. 9.

between third & fourth Streets, where Orders in the Printing & Foundery Lines are received & carefully executed by B. F. Bache.[17]

The types marked with an asterisk, cast from French matrices, failed to attract American printers. Bache himself seems to have realized this inasmuch as most of the type in his specimen comprised Caslon characters. Therefore, it may be a consideration that his own lack of punchcutting skill was only one of other conditions unfavorable to business; another, perhaps the more important, lies in Franklin's selection of French designs. If the matrices had been purchased in England or Scotland, or if Bache had been aggressive enough to alter the product of the foundry, Binny & Ronaldson might have lost their monopoly.

Instead of remedying the state of affairs, Bache turned his attention to book and newspaper work, achieving a reputation with his well-known newspaper, the *Aurora*. At his death in the yellow fever epidemic of 1798, his wife Margaret took charge of his firm, and the paper was published for his heirs.[18] Two years later Margaret married William Duane, editor of the *Aurora*. With Duane as publisher, the *Aurora* continued hand in hand with the printing office, but the foundry remained dormant. Nevertheless, Duane hoped for its revival. In 1802 some per-

[17] *A Specimen of Printing Types Belonging to Benjamin Franklin Bache's Printing Office, Philadelphia* (n.d.), p. 3. Facsimile in NNC-Typ.

[18] Clarence S. Brigham, *History and Bibliography of American Newspapers, 1690–1820* (Worcester, Mass., 1947), II, 891.

BENJAMIN FRANKLIN BACHE's SPECIMEN.

*Pica Rom.

Tandem aliquando, Quirites ! L. Catilinam furentem audacia, fcelus anhelantem, peftem patriæ nefarie molientem, vobis atque huic urbi ferrum flammamque minitantem ex urbe vel ejecimus, vel emifimus, vel ipfum egredientem verbis profecuti fumus. Abiit, exceffit, evafit, erupit. Nulla jam pernicies
ABCDEFGHIJKLMNOPQRSTUVWXYZÆŒ.

*Small Pica Rom.

Tandem aliquando, Quirites ! L. Catilinam furentem audacia, fcelus anhelantem, peftem patriæ nefarie molienten, vobis atque huic urbi ferrum flammamque minitantem, ex urbe vel ejecimus, vel emifimus, vel ipfum egredientem verbis profecuti fumus. Abiit, exceffit, evafit, eruentem verbis profecuti fumus. Abiit, exceffit, evafit, eru-
ABCDEFGHIJKLMNOPQRSTUVWXYZŒ.

*Pica Ital.

Tandem aliquando, Quirites ! L. Catilinam furentem audacia, fcelus anhelantem, peftem patrie nefarie molientem, vobis atque huic urbi ferrum flammamque minitantem, ex urbe vel ejcimus, vel emifimus, vel ipfum egredientem verbis profecuti fumus. Abiit, exceffit, eva-
ABCDEFGHIJKLMNOPQRSTUVWXYZÆ Œ.

*Small Pica Ital.

Tandem aliquando, Quirites ! L. Catilinam furentem audacia, fcelus anhelantem, peftem patriæ nefarie molientem, vobis atque huic urbi ferrum flammamque minitantem, ex urbe vel ejecimus, vel emifimus, vel ipfum egredientem verbis profecuti fumus. Abiit, ecceffit, evafit, egredientem verbis profecuti fumus. Abiit, ecceffit, evafit,
ABCDEFGHIJKLMNOPQRSTUVWXYZÆŒ.

Plate 10 – Benjamin Franklin Bache, c. 1790

son, most likely Duane himself who was then in Washington attempting to get the government printing contract, persuaded Congress to propose an increase in the duty on imported types from 12½ per cent ad valorem to 20 per cent. At the same time, in response to the petition of Binny & Ronaldson, Congress proposed to eliminate the duty on antimony.

Duane, anticipating that these revisions might help restore his foundry, indiscreetly publicized them in the *Aurora*. Almost instantaneously the printing and book trades in six cities called mass meetings and bombarded Congress with petitions of protest.[19]

Duane fought the campaign in his columns, but he could not defeat the rapidly organized lobby. In the final version of the bill Congress exempted antimony from duty and retained the lower rate of duty on type. Outwitted in his attempt to obtain greater tariff protection, Duane abandoned the foundry. In 1806 the executors of B. F. Bache's estate offered the typefounding equipment to Binny & Ronaldson who, it will be recalled, quickly accepted. Although Binny & Ronaldson apparently did little if any casting from the matrices, Binny, as will be discussed later, may have drawn some helpful conclusions from the construction of the casting equipment. At present thirty of the Franklin matrices, probably overlooked at the time of transfer, may be seen at the Massachusetts Historical Society. They

[19] Silver, *SB*, III, 210–28.

were presented to the Society in 1838 by William J. Duane.[20]

A shred of evidence about another typefoundry existing at the same time as Franklin's is given in a sentence in the diary of one of the most distinguished scholars of the period, William Bentley of Salem, Massachusetts: "April 30 [1787]. . . . The Printer Mr. Mycall gave me some Types from his own Foundery which did him honor."[21] John Mycall (c. 1750–1833), born in Worcester, England, printed and published in Newburyport, Massachusetts, between 1775 and 1794.[22] Thomas speaks of him as "a man of great ingenuity," but makes no mention of him as a typefounder.[23] Nor has a search of probable sources revealed any additional information. Because Bentley was interested in the craft of printing, his statement must be considered while awaiting verification.

Still another Philadelphia printer besides Franklin turned typefounder. About 1792–McCulloch thought it might have been earlier–Francis Bailey purchased at least one font of matrices from Jacob Bay.[24] Bailey, born in Lancaster County, Pennsylvania, about 1735, became a carpenter's apprentice but left to learn printing in Peter Miller's shop at Ephrata. For a time Bailey printed on his own in

[20] Information in a letter from Malcolm Freiberg, Massachusetts Historical Society, Jan. 8, 1963.

[21] *The Diary of William Bentley, D. D.* (Salem, Mass., 1905), I, 60–61.

[22] American Antiquarian Society, Printers File.

[23] Thomas, *Hist. of Print.*, I, 180.

[24] *McCulloch*, pp. 182, 233.

Lancaster before moving to Philadelphia, where he resumed printing in 1778.[25] Increasingly fascinated by mechanics, he often visited Bay's foundry not only to buy type, but to observe; there Bailey "received his insight to type casting."[26] He probably acquired the matrices from Bay during the latter's insolvency. Other equipment, it will be remembered, was obtained from John Baine.

In his foundry Bailey constructed part of the equipment himself, at times inventing devices, for "as a mechanician," states Thomas, "he was celebrated."[27] He then began to cast type chiefly for his own use, making no special attempt to market it in quantity. Bailey himself often cut and engraved ornaments and cuts, but when additional matrices were needed, he frequently hired Frederic Geyer as punchcutter.[28] It is also known that Jacob Kempfer cast from Bay's matrices the letters which appeared in a Bailey edition of a Testament.[29] McCulloch cites the fact that Bailey's standing edition of a bourgeois Testament, in Bailey's type, was sold to Mathew Carey.[30] The bill of sale, at present in the American Antiquarian Society, is dated April 10, 1811 and reads: "One testament standing in Chases with Rack and letter boards @ $800." Bailey discontinued typefounding when he moved to his farm

[25] American Antiquarian Society. Printers File; H. Glenn Brown and Maude O. Brown, *A Directory of the Book-Arts and Book Trade in Philadelphia to 1820* (New York, 1950), p. 15.
[26] *McCulloch*, pp. 182, 233–34.
[27] Thomas, *Hist. of Print.*, I, 287.
[28] *McCulloch*, p. 234.   [29] *Ibid.*   [30] *Ibid.*, p. 104.

at Octoraro, Pennsylvania, in 1802. He came out of
retirement in 1809 with the hope of establishing his
son Andrew in a newly activated business in Philadelphia.[31] A contemporary judgment, "Some founts
have been cast, but the promise is not great," sums
up their predicament.[32] Bailey's death at Philadelphia in 1815 ended the story of this foundry.[33]

In the final decade of the eighteenth century one
other foundry was certainly casting and another
may possibly have been in operation. The latter, if
it did exist, was set up at Fairhaven, Vermont, by
Matthew Lyon about 1793. Two of Lyon's biogra-
phers alleged that he cast type in his own foundry,
but no evidence has been cited.[34] Instead, as Skillin
points out, there is a hint of the lack of a foundry:
on October 26, 1796, Lyon's publication, the *Farmer's Library*, could not print all the winning lottery
numbers because of a "want of figures."[35] It may be
conjectured that Lyon's foundry was a biographical
fancy. The other foundry was succinctly described
by McCulloch:

Conden and Harrison commenced a foundry in Philadelphia about the same time as Binny and Ronaldson; but the attempt proved abortive. B. and R. purchased some of their materials. But these, as well as
most other purchased apparatus, were of little serv-

[31] *Ibid.*, p. 98.   [32] *Ibid.*
[33] American Antiquarian Society. Printers File.
[34] Tom Walter Campbell, *Two Fighters and Two Fines*
(Little Rock, 1941), pp. 30–31; J. Fairfax McLaughlin,
"A Picturesque Politician of Jefferson's Time," *Century
Illus. Monthly*, LXV (1903), 933.
[35] Information in a letter from Glenn B. Skillin, April
10, 1962.

ice. The fashion and figure of the type improved so rapidly that the old materials soon became like lumber and trash.[36]

Furthermore, the Philadelphia directory for 1797 contains a listing for Timothy Harrison, typefounder, at the corner of Cherry and North.

At the outset of the nineteenth century a more effective foundry was established in Baltimore by Samuel Sower, a member of a family distinguished in the annals of American printing. Grandson of the first Christopher Sower and tenth son of the second, Samuel, born March 20, 1767, grew up in the robust fashion of those days, mastering a combination of skills. In his youth he settled at Chestnut Hill, Pennsylvania, as a house carpenter, but shortly afterward became an apothecary as well as a printer. At Chestnut Hill, from 1791 until 1794, the year in which he moved to Philadelphia, he issued at least twelve books and pamphlets from his press. Sower could not have remained in Philadelphia for more than about a year, however, for on March 27, 1795, he announced the opening of a German and English printing office in Baltimore.[37] He began with job work and the publication of a German weekly paper, but within a few years added bookbinding. In 1802 the Baltimore directory listed him as "book printer and bookseller."

About 1804 Sower commenced typefounding in

[36] *McCulloch*, p. 187.
[37] Biographical information about Samuel Sower is in A. Rachel Minick, *A History of Printing in Maryland, 1791–1800* (Baltimore, 1949), pp. 100–110.

copartnership with William Gwynn, later the proprietor of the *Federal Gazette*. Gwynn, a silent partner, apparently furnished the capital for the business conducted as Samuel Sower & Co., also known,
aside from its original name, as the Baltimore Type
Foundry.[38] Probably formal organization merely
served to increase Sower's activities, for having
grown up in a family of typefounders, he understood
the craft well enough to cast for his own use, and
presumably had done so before this. (Evans
thought that a cut of Hermes in a Sower publication
of 1796 was perhaps cast in the Sower shop.[39]) In
addition, his elder brother, Christopher Sower III,
had arrived in the spring of 1799 to join him in typefounding, but as he died in July of that same year,
expansion had had to await the coming of Gwynn.[40]

Sower's own equipment was increased in 1806
through purchase of the Fox foundry from Eman-
uel, son of Justus, thus returning part of the Sower
family possessions to the descendant. Unfortunately, Samuel found them inadequate because, according to McCulloch, the matrices "were fabri-
cated of brass, which heats too soon, and during the
casting of a large fount, are apt to vary their exten-
sion."[41] This may have impeded Sower's production, but it did not inhibit it. Sower's type was so

[38] *McCulloch*, p. 162; Oswald Seidensticker, "Synopsis
of Prof. O. Seidensticker's Address," in Society for the History of the Germans in Maryland, *Report 3d.* (Baltimore,
1888–89), pp. 15–16; Rollo G. Silver, *The Baltimore Book
Trade, 1800–1825* (New York, 1953), p. 15.
[39] Charles Evans, *American Bibliography* (Chicago,
1929), X, 148.
[40] Minick, *A History*, pp. 106–7.
[41] *McCulloch*, p. 169.

well received that he withdrew from printing and bookselling to supervise his rapidly developing business. His rather turbulent prosperity is described in a letter of December 7, 1808:

I am chained down (to business) closer than ever, for I am employing the two Kempfers, a journeyman and a young learner, besides the stamp cutter, and six or seven apprentices, and expect to employ one or two more journeymen.–My partner will not bother himself with business, having invested between $7000 and $8000 in the business and built for me a home costing at least $3000. I see him not more than once a month and he leaves everything in my hands to manage, saying if he had not the utmost confidence in me, he should not have gone into it.–The business of type founding is making great strides,–orders are pouring in from everywhere, so that we cannot fill the half of them. We have undertaken to cast the smallest type that have yet been used in the world. You may judge of its fineness when it takes 4–5000 spaces to weigh one pound. Of this type we have an order from New York for 300 pounds for a Bible.–I send Brother David a Catalogue containing almost all the type we have had engraved and you may never have looked upon a neater specimen of type. We have received an order from Albany for a note-type for a book of hymns, 1500 pounds for $2587. If we could get Antimony enough, we could have work for twelve founders. I am working night and day. We have eleven boys and six journeymen at work and orders for 5000 pounds type.[42]

Of the "two Kempfers," Jacob, "typefounder," died about 1818; a "Joseph Kampher," "type dresser," is

[42] Seidensticker, "Synopsis," pp. 15–16.

listed in the Baltimore directory for 1822–23.[43] The "stamp cutter" most likely was Christian Gobrecht who has been identified as the engraver who "cut the type punches for the Baltimore Foundery."[44] Gobrecht, a talented medallist and inventor of engraving tools, is also reported by McCulloch as an employee of the foundry.[45]

Two other items in Sower's letter command attention: the diamond type and the "Catalogue." His contemporary, Isaiah Thomas, must have rated the casting of diamond, in both roman and italic, as Sower's superior achievement because he refers to no other.[46] The type, doubtless intended for Bible use, may be seen in an edition of the Bible printed by Sower's nephew, Brooke W. Sower, and published by John Hagerty in 1812.[47] This volume bears a statement on the title page declaring it to be the first American diamond edition. The "Catalogue" is, at present, one of the lacunae in lists of available type specimen books. A copy, dated 1808, was listed in the catalogue of the library of the Typothetae, published in 1896, with an annotation indicating the fact that the "specimens include a diamond, the first cast in this country."[48]

[43] Silver, *Baltimore Book Trade*, p. 37.

[44] *Federal Gazette*, July 1, 1813.

[45] George C. Groce and David H. Wallace, *The New-York Historical Society's Dictionary of Artists in America* (New Haven, 1957), p. 263; *McCulloch*, p. 162.

[46] Thomas, *Hist. of Print.*, I, 285.

[47] *McCulloch*, p. 162; Margaret T. Hills, *The English Bible in America* (New York, 1961), p. 37.

[48] *Catalogue of the Books in the Library of The Typothetae of the City of New York* (New York, 1896), p. 123.

On December 25, 1809, the Baltimore *American* announced that it would only use type from the Baltimore Type Foundry for, at last, the foundry had come into its own. Although, as with Binny & Ronaldson, the antimony shortage continued to be an impediment more and more extreme as war began, Sower did obtain a large supply from France which enabled him to advertise in 1812 that he was ready to execute orders for sizes from diamond to French canon, including music, script, and German text.[49] About the same time, the Baltimore *Federal Gazette* became a customer, beginning an association which lasted at least until 1822; this was confirmed by the newspaper when it announced in that year that it had been printed wholly from Baltimore Type Foundry type during the decade.[50]

Meanwhile, when relative economic stability emerged after the wartime inflationary period, other foundries in the growing cities began to compete for the market. Sower's time of success drew to an end as he found himself restricted from activity by his failing eyesight and poor health.[51] Inevitably his volume of business declined, but the Baltimore Type Foundry remained, though its great days were over. After Sower's death in Baltimore October 12, 1820, his son-in-law, Richard B. Spalding, continued the business.[52] Spalding, a merchant, maintained it by supplying local printers as well as

[49] *Federal Gazette*, March 19, 1812.
[50] *Federal Gazette*, Jan. 2, 1822.
[51] Seidensticker, "Synopsis," p. 16.
[52] Silver, *Baltimore Book Trade*, p. 51.

the *Federal Gazette*, which in 1825 announced new type from the foundry.[53] Under a succession of owners, the Baltimore Type Foundry survived until it became part of the American Type Founders Company in 1892.

That Sower could establish himself as a type-founder was due to an intuitive understanding of economics and to his control of the craftsmanship of his product. He was a prototype of the early nineteenth-century manager who was free, before the industrial revolution began, to adapt himself to every situation, to hire or fire, to go out after orders himself, and was able without hindrance to run his own shop. But this dynamism, while prevalent in our early history, was not always present, as is shown by the example of the Scotch typefounder, Robert Lothian, who set up a foundry in New York in 1806, but was unsuccessful.

There is quite a bit of mystery about Robert Lothian. McCulloch calls him "the once rev. Mr. Lothian," but his name cannot be found in the printed church records of Scotland.[54] He is said by McCulloch to have had a history "as interesting and diversified" as that of any other founder. David Bruce, Jr., compounds the confusion by mentioning him as Dr. Robert Lothian.[55] At any rate, he is listed as a typefounder in the Edinburgh directories of 1804, 1805, and 1806. He left Edinburgh for New

---

[53] *Federal Gazette*, July 1, 1825.
[54] *McCulloch*, p. 185.
[55] *Ibid.;* D[avid] B[ruce], [Jr.], "Mr. George Buxton Lothian," *Typographic Messenger*, II (Nov. 1866), 1; hereinafter cited as *Bruce-Lothian*.

York where he issued a type specimen in 1806.[56] It is reasonable to believe, because the transition occurred in a comparatively short time, that the specimen with the New York imprint had been prepared, if not issued, in Edinburgh. At present, no Edinburgh specimen can be located for corroborative proof. Perhaps the study by William Bentinck-Smith will clarify the reasons for Lothian's failure within a period of four years. Lothian sold his equipment in 1810 to Binny & Ronaldson and died shortly afterwards.[57]

Robert Lothian's son, George Buxton Lothian, suffered from a dichotomy in personality that brought misery in his life as well as in business. There seemed to be a continual struggle between the rigid demands of an excellent mind and a sense of outrage at the less than perfect results he was able to achieve under the conditions in which he found himself. As his impatience grew, so did violence, until it all but mastered him. Feeling misunderstood, such a man goes from place to place, and so did Lothian. In the year his father sold out, he left a Philadelphia bookseller to work in the New York typefoundry of John Watts.[58] When Watts began stereotyping, young Lothian learned that craft as well, but soon the basic anger and insecurity welled up, and after a disagreement over "real or supposed injuries," Lothian went to jail.[59] David

[56] Information in a communication from Ralph Green, March 28, 1952.
[57] *Am. Dict. Print.*, p. 351.   [58] *Bruce-Lothian*, p. 1.
[59] *Ibid.*

Bruce, Jr., who wrote a sympathetic memoir, said:

The organization, or rather disorganization, of Mr. Lothian's mental qualities, although admitted as highly intellectual, was certainly very unbalanced— so much so, at times, that it required the exercise of all the charity and forbearance of his friends to bear with his unreasonable outbreaks of temper. Although his conversational powers generally rendered him quite companionable, there was no certainty how long this might last. His antipathies against certain persons and things were so crochety, that not unfrequently a very pleasant interview terminated in high words or a row.[60]

After a two-year stint as stereotype finisher for Collins & Hanna, he went to Pittsburgh, where he established a typefoundry in 1819.[61] Assisted by Peter C. Cortelyou, later a well-known New York typefounder, he cast type, but this undertaking lasted less than a year.[62] Lothian returned to New York in financial trouble. David & George Bruce bought his equipment and employed him only to find that the excellent workman was "a very disagreeable shopmate."[63] He asked the Bruces for a release in order to go on the stage—an ambition which he had possessed since the time he took part in amateur theatricals in Philadelphia.

When a series of elocution lessons proved too

[60] *Ibid.*
[61] *Ibid.;* information in a letter from Prudence B. Trimble, Historical Society of Western Pennsylvania, May 11, 1961.
[62] Theodore Low De Vinne, *The Practice of Typography ...Plain Printing Types* (New York, 1900), p. 104.
[63] *Bruce-Lothian*, p. 1.

confining for his undisciplined memory, though his characterization was professional, he returned to typefounding. About 1822 he supplied type in small amounts to the Harper brothers, and then, to increase the size of his plant, entered into partnership with Alfred Pell, an investor, under the firm name of Lothian & Pell. This firm appears in only one New York directory—that of 1825–26; its short life ended when there was an argument after which "ground and lofty tumbling ensued."[64] Lothian's interest was purchased by William Hagar.[65] About 1829 Lothian resumed manufacturing for the Harpers who, as customers, also had to contend with his unstable personality:

He continued manufacturing for the Messrs. Harper—these gentlemen bearing with all his taunts, sarcasms, and wormwood remarks with Christian meekness and charity, perfectly satisfied to bear all with philosophical calmness, provided he continued to furnish them with well manufactured type; which he certainly did. The excellence of his manufactured articles, the harmony of his several faces, were admitted by all; but the capriciousness of temper which characterized his intercourse with customers had the effect of limiting his business to a very narrow scope.[66]

With his grave, respectful manner, Bruce, in 1866, also recalled Lothian's endurance under actual stress:

Again, when it is considered that the herculian task of establishing a type-foundry without capital was

[64] *Ibid.*   [65] *Ibid.*   [66] *Ibid.*

undertaken by one of so peculiar an organization; that the minutest details were necessarily attended to by himself; that the stupidity of inefficient boy-labor (necessary, in his case, on the score of economy,) where skilled workmen were required, was a constant source of irritation; that under all these peculiar difficulties, his exquisite sense of the harmonious and beautiful in type must be (and was) carried out by him—the practical type-founder, knowing how to sympathize with him, will cheerfully throw the mantle of oblivion over most of his faults. Ever on the alert to conduct his business with the greatest economy, he added many improved methods of manufacture which hold their place to this day. He was one of the experimental pioneers in machine type-casting and type-rubbing, and the invention of the method now used of kerning type. There were three subjects which were inexhaustible with him—the stage, music, and type-founding; and should any one be so fortunate as to harmonize with him on any or all of these subjects, every thing might go well between them.[67]

Sadly, this extraordinarily sensitive man had to suffer in addition to the burden of his temperament the loss of wife, sons, and daughters. At his death, aged fifty-seven, on August 14, 1850, he left, ironically, a "handsome competency judiciously bequeathed."[68]

Apart from the increase in the number of typefounders, the introduction of stereotyping in the second decade of the nineteenth century made an

[67] *Ibid.*, pp. 1–2.
[68] *Ibid.*, p. 2; New York *Daily Tribune*, Aug. 15, 1850.

appreciable change in business competition. The promising new process immediately attracted the attention of all typefounders, some of whom added stereotyping to their techniques. Occasionally others made it their major, if not their total venture. Adorinam Chandler's shop is an example of this. Listed as a typefounder in the New York directory of 1820, he appears in subsequent directories as a stereotype founder. His first known specimen, dated 1820, is a *Specimen of Ornamental Types and Embellishments* consisting of more embellishments than type.[69] His second, *Specimen of Ornamental Type and Printing Ornaments* (1822), includes a blunt "Notice" to come and buy:

The ornamental types exhibited in this specimen are cast in stereotype plates, and the letters separately fixed to wooden bottoms. A great quantity of this kind of job type has been in use for three years past, and those who have tried it, speak decidedly in its favour. Printers are left to judge for themselves, whether it is not a saving to buy this, instead of giving forty-two cents per pound for type metal. It is warranted to last as long as any job type cast in the United States. It will be made up in founts to suit purchasers, at eighteen cents per letter.[70]

Chandler's price may be compared with James Ronaldson's price list of January 1, 1822, wherein plain two-line letter is listed at 42 cents per pound, orna-

[69] *Specimen of Ornamental Types and Embellishments* (New York, 1820). Copy in PPAmP.
[70] *Specimen of Ornamental Type and Printing Ornaments* (New York, 1822), p. 1. Copy in NNC-Typ.

mented two-line letter at 90 cents, and seven-line pica shaded at 55 cents.[71] Chandler's specimen includes six- and eight-line pica ornamented (Plate 11).

Beneath the "Notice" in the specimen, Chandler added a self-assured estimate of the virtues of his product:

Stereotyping.

The principal objections which have been urged against stereotype plates are the inequality of their thickness, unevenness of their surface, &c. and the consequent difficulty of obtaining a fair impression from them. The subscriber, having spared no pains in obtaining a knowledge of, and adopting the best practical operations in this business, together with essential improvements, which some years experience has suggested, feels justified in assuring those whom it may concern, that the plates cast at his foundry are not surpassed by those from any other foundry either in Europe or America. Works of several hundred pages, on small type, have been put to press with as little difficulty, as respects *overlaying* and *register*, as the same work would require if done on separate type.

All orders for stereotyping will be thankfully received, and executed with despatch, on the most accommodating terms.[72]

Chandler's firm is discussed here because it represents a specialized foundry; other firms which carried on both processes as "type and stereotype founders" will be treated in another chapter.

[71] *Specimen of Printing Type* (Philadelphia, 1822), p. 107.
[72] *Specimen of Ornamental Type*, p. 1.

EIGHT LINES PICA ORNAMENTED.

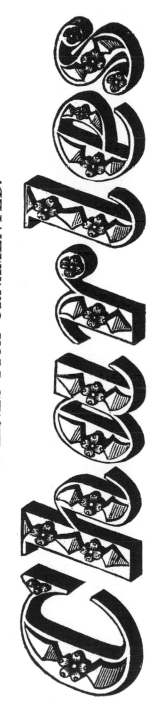

* Casts from the original engravings of this type, can be obtained only at A. Chandler's Foundry.

Plate 11 – Adorinam Chandler, 1822

These individualistic founders of the period—
Bailey, Sower, Lothian—were self-directed workmen who, planning on a small scale, designed and
conducted their businesses on the premise that the
craftsmanship of their shops must be of the highest
standard instead of, as later happened, the poorest
the market could bear. Although they were nowhere
as prosperous as the later captains of industry, their
ethical considerations were indispensable to the new
democracy.

GROWTH

AND EXPANSION

At the end of the eighteenth century the firm of
Binny & Ronaldson of Philadelphia was the only
one in America competent enough to give immediate
and continuous service to its customers. In other
parts of the country printers who needed type in an
emergency depended upon the good will of their
competitors in an adventitious system of borrowing
and lending. As an illustration, when Thomas &
Andrews set the text of Samuel Webber's *Mathe-
matics* (1801), they discovered they were short of
type, so they had to search for it in four Massachusetts towns. Joseph T. Buckingham, the compositor
on this job, recalled their predicament: "Much time
was spent in borrowing arithmetical and algebraical
characters from other offices. I believe there was

scarcely a fount of letter in Boston, Worcester, Charlestown and Cambridge, that was not laid under contribution;—for then there was no typefoundery here that could be called upon to supply deficiencies."[1] While such interdependence could prevail in a simplified economy, the increased population with its demands for reading matter gave rise to a larger number of printing offices. These, in turn, were able to provide enough support to maintain local foundries, particularly in the larger cities.

The first successful New York foundry, E. White & Co., began about 1811, a short time after Robert Lothian sold his equipment to Binny & Ronaldson. It is known that White was born in Bolton, Connecticut, on July 27, 1773, but the first twenty years of his life cannot be accurately traced.[2] Apparently he came into the trade without having served time as an apprentice, simply motivated by the idea of inventing a machine which would make his fortune. It was in 1794, stated David Bruce, Jr., that Elihu White and William Wing began work in Hartford, Connecticut, on the design of a typecasting machine.[3] Another date is supplied by the *American Dictionary of Printing and Bookmaking:* "In 1805, in concert with another inventor named Wing, he began casting types at Hartford, but as they had no one to instruct them in many of the most common operations of a type-foundry their progress for a

[1] Joseph T. Buckingham, *Personal Memoirs* (Boston, 1852), I, 51.
[2] *Am. Dict. Print.*, p. 582.
[3] Bruce, *Typ. Mess.*, III (Nov. 1867), 1.

long time was slow. Their plan was to cast a number of types together, and then separate them."[4]

Both sources agreed that the inventors had only a scrappy knowledge of typefounding. Native mechanical ability plus audacity devised a machine which was patented August 28, 1805.[5] In October of the following year, "Elihu White, of Threadneedle Street, in the City of London" received an English patent for the same or a similar machine.[6] All that can be surmised from White's English journey is that he must have been adequately financed, and that he hoped to capture the English market. The machine turned out to be impractical. As he now had a large investment to salvage, White decided that he had experimented enough to set up a foundry employing the procedures then in use. No sooner did he begin to work than he discovered that with all their experience, neither he nor his associates knew much about the common type-mold. This would have been a major setback to a lesser man, for the only place in the United States to learn about a type-mold was in the Binny & Ronaldson factory, where, to prevent competition, admission was refused to visitors.

The ingenious Yankee resorted to a questionable stratagem: he sent an employee, Edwin Starr, to apply for work at the Philadelphia foundry. Starr, posing as a malcontent, told Binny and Ronaldson that White had succeeded in improving his machine

[4] *Am. Dict. Print.*, p. 582.
[5] Bruce, *Typ. Mess.*, III (Nov. 1867), 1.
[6] *White's Specification* (London, 1856), p. 1.

and hinted that he would be willing to exchange its secrets for a job with them. As the partners deliberated, a letter arrived from White with a complaint about his renegade employee and an expression of faith that his competitors, as honorable men, would not encourage Starr to violate any confidence. In conclusion, he warned them against using any of his devices. The combination of Starr's tale and White's corroborative letter completely fooled Binny and Ronaldson and, in glee at the prospect of copying the wonderful new invention, they hired Starr. The latter, according to Bruce, "freely communicated the wonders of this type-casting abortion in all its crudeness, and received in return all he wanted—a glance at a common type-mold."[7] Quickly he returned to Hartford with the desired information.[8]

The White and Wing foundry probably began in 1808, certainly before December 1809, when their advertisement for old metal appeared in the *American Mercury*.[9] The realization of the Hartford shop quieted White's ambitious drive only for a short while. His tireless mind sought wider adventures, especially a move to New York City where opportunities were greater in a large population which had no foundry. The decision to leave Hartford was not impulsive; the type produced there appeared good enough to attract New York printers, but he had to

[7] Bruce, *Typ. Mess.*, III (Nov. 1867), 1–2.
[8] *Ibid.*, p. 2.
[9] *American Mercury*, Dec. 28, 1809. This information was supplied by Thompson R. Harlow.

move rapidly, if at all, as the country seemed on the verge of war. When at last the negotiations for the New York site were completed, his move was welcomed by at least one printer in the area. In October 1811, the *Long Island Star* complimented the newcomer:

We are happy to add to the above interesting information, that the Type Foundry of Messrs. White & Co. of Hartford, Ct., is shortly to be removed to New York. We may therefore expect the printers of this section of the Union to be less subjected to impositions than heretofore. This foundry has recently produced type of a peculiarly beautiful cut, and well adapted to service. New York, we may confidently expect, will soon rival her sister cities in these first of all arts.[10]

White's decision proved wise; the printers liked his faces and he soon enjoyed a large trade. Within a short time he issued the *Specimen of Printing Types from the Foundry of E. White & Co.* (1812), a modest pamphlet which promised more in future editions:

In offering to the public this small specimen of their type, the proprietors of the New-York Foundry have briefly to observe, that the infancy of their establishment prevents their exhibiting a more extensive variety at this time; but their exertions, aided by the talents and taste of their own country, shall not be wanting to embrace every kind of letter and ornament that the best foundries of Europe can produce. They trust, however, that on comparing these sam-

[10] Quoted in J. Munsell, *The Typographical Miscellany* (Albany, 1850), p. 114.

Quousque tandem abutere, Catilina, patientia nostra? quamdiu nos etiam furor iste tuus eludet? quem ad finem sese effrenata jactabit audacia? nihilne te nocturnum præsidium palatii, nihil urbis vigiliæ, nihil timor populi, nihil consensus bonorum omnium, nihil hic munitissimus habendi senatus locus, nihil horum ora vultusque moverunt? patere tua consilia non sentis? constrictam jam omnium horum conscientia teneri conjurationem tuam non vides? quid proxima, quid superiore nocte egeris, ubi fueris, quos convocaveris, quid consilii ceperis, quem nostrum ignorare arbitraris? O tempora, o mores! Senatus hoc intelligit, consul videt: hic tamen vivit. Vivit? imo vero etiam in Senatum venit: fit publici consilii particeps: notat et designat oculis ad cædem

ABCDEFGHIJKLMNOPQRSTUVWXYZ&

ABCDEFGHIJKLMNOPQRSTUVWXYZÆŒ

1234567890

Quousque tandem abutere, Catilina, patientia nostra? quamdiu nos etiam furor iste tuus eludet? quem ad finem sese effrenata jactabit audacia? nihilne te nocturnum præsidium palatii, nihil urbis vigiliæ, nihil timor populi, nihil consensus bonorum omnium, nihil hic munitissimus habendi senatus locus, nihil horum ora vultusque moverunt? patere tua consilia non sentis? constrictam jam omnium horum conscientia teneri conjurationem tuam non vides? quid proxima, quid superiore nocte egeris, ubi fueris, quos convocaveris, quid consilii ceperis, quem nostrum ignorare arbitraris? O tempora, o mores! Senatus hoc intelligit, consul videt: hic tamen vivit.

ABCDEFGHIJKLMNOPQRSTUVWXYZ
ÆŒ

Plate 12 – E. White & Co., 1812

Quousque tandem abutere, Catilina, patientia nostra? quamdiu nos etiam furor iste tuus eludet? quem ad finem sese effrenata jactabit audacia? nihilne te nocturnum præsidium palatii, nihil urbis vigiliæ, nihil timor populi, nihil consensus bonorum omnium, nihil hic munitissimus habendi senatus locus, nihil horum ora vultusque moverunt? patere tua consilia non sentis? constrictam jam omnium horum conscientia teneri conjurationem

ABCDEFGHIJKLMNOPQRSTUV

ABCDEFGHIJKLMNOPQRSTUVWXYZÆŒ

$ 1234567890

Quousque tandem abutere, Catilina, patientia nostra? quamdiu nos etiam furor iste tuus eludet? quem ad finem sese effrenata jactabit audacia? nihilne te nocturnum præsidium palatii, nihil consensus bonorum omnium, nihil hic munitissimus habendi senatus locus, nihil horum ora vultusque moverunt? patere

ABCDEFGHIJKLMNOPQRSTUV WXYZÆŒ&

Plate 13 – E. White & Co., 1812

ples with others, their establishment will be found to merit encouragement from the printers of the United States; and such orders as they may please to forward will meet with the most prompt attention; the proprietors being determined to render their establishment worthy of a liberal patronage.[11]

This nationalistic optimism, quite in the style of an adolescent America, preceded a showing of sizes ranging from great primer to nonpareil as well as two-line letters and flowers. As would be expected White displayed a useful face, fairly priced—55 cents for pica, 66 cents for long primer, 86 cents for brevier[12] (Plates 12, 13).

The new development of stereotyping excited White's ambition. In association with his brother Julius he organized a company in 1815 under the name of E. & J. White, one of their first jobs being a brevier Bible for the New-York Bible Society which appeared in the following year.[13] After the American Bible Society was founded in 1816, E. & J. White stereotyped a long primer Bible which that Society published in 1817 or 1818.[14] One can infer from this second order that he not only had the hardihood to attempt difficult jobs but also the talent to complete them satisfactorily in new techniques.

Elihu White's typefounding business also re-

[11] *Specimen of Printing Types from the Foundry of E. White & Co.* (New York, 1812), pp. 1–2. Copy in NNC-Typ.
[12] *Ibid.*, p. 2.
[13] *Am. Dict. Print.*, p. 583; Hills, *English Bible*, p. 50.
[14] Hills, *English Bible*, p. 57.

mained on a sure footing despite losses of personnel. Edwin Starr joined his brothers about 1812 to start a competitive foundry nearby.[15] William Wing, who probably accompanied White in the move from Hartford, died, aged 56, at Saybrook, Connecticut, in December 1817.[16] Wing's departure may have prompted White to omit the "& Co." from the firm name on the cover of the 1817 specimen book. Now he exhibited a more extensive assortment than in 1812, including two sizes of Greek, small pica and long primer, as well as a specimen of stereotyping by E. & J. White[17] (Plates 14, 15). Prices duplicated those of 1812 for the sizes which appeared in both books.

The first American printing manual, C. S. Van Winkle's *Printers' Guide* of 1818, presented at the end of the text another White specimen which included the popular sizes and, in a prefatory note, referred the reader to the separate specimen for "all the sizes, from ten lines pica down to pearl, inclusive."[18] The note concluded with the guarantee that "Mr. W. has also made arrangements which will enable him to supply, at a short notice, any articles that may be ordered by the trade, such as presses, cases, ink, paper, chases, composing sticks, furniture, &c."[19] White's next specimen, three years later,

[15] Bruce, *Typ. Mess.*, III (Nov. 1867), 2.
[16] *Courant*, Dec. 9, 1817. This information was supplied by Thompson R. Harlow.
[17] *A Specimen of Printing Types from the Foundry of E. White* (New York, 1817). Copy in NNC-Typ.
[18] C. S. Van Winkle, *Printers' Guide* (New York, 1818), p. 232.
[19] *Ibid.*

Quousque tandem abutere, Catilina, patientia nostra? quamdiu nos etiam furor iste tuus eludet? quem ad finem sese effrenata jactabit audacia? nihilne te nocturnum praesidium palatii, nihil urbis vigiliae, nihil timor populi, nihil consensus bonorum omnium, nihil hic munitissimus habendi senatus locus, nihil horum ora vultusque moverunt? patere tua consilia non sentis? constrictam jam omnium horum conscientia teneri conjurationem tuam non vides? quid proxima, quid superiore nocte egeris, ubi fueris, quos convocaveris, quid consilii ceperis, quem nostrum ignorare arbitraris? O tempora, o mores! Senatus hoc intelligit, consul videt: hic tamen vivit. Vivit? imo vero etiam in senatum venit: fit publici consilii particeps: notat et

ABCDEFGHIJKLMNOPQRSTUVWXYZ

ABCDEFGHIJKLMNOPQRSTUVWXYZÆŒ

1234567890

$\frac{1\ 2\ 3\ 4\ 5\ 6\ 7\ 8\ 9\ 0}{1\ 2\ 3\ 4\ 5\ 6\ 7\ 8\ 9\ 0}$

Quousque tandem abutere, Catilina, patientia nostra? quamdiu nos etiam furor iste tuus eludet? quem ad finem sese effrenata jactabit audacia? nihilne te nocturnum praesidium palatii, nihil urbis vigiliae, nihil timor populi, nihil consensus bonorum omnium, nihil hic munitissimus habendi senatus locus, nihil horum ora vultusque moverunt? patere tua consilia non sentis? constrictam jam omnium horum conscientia teneri conjurationem tuam non vides? quid proxima, quid superiore nocte egeris, ubi fueris, quos convocaveris, quid consilii ceperis, quem nostrum ignorare arbitraris? O tempora, o mores! Senatus hoc intelligit, consul videt: hic tamen vivit. Vivit? imo vero etiam in senatum venit: fit publici consilii particeps: notat et designat oculis ad caedem unumquemque nostrum. Nos autem viri fortes satisfacere reipublicae, videmur, si

ABCDEFGHIJKLMNOPQRSTUV WXYZ ÆŒ

E. White.   New-York.

Plate 14 – Elihu White, 1817

Pica No. 3.

Quousque tandem abutere, Catilina, patientia nostra? quamdiu nos etiam furor iste tuus eludet? quem ad finem sese effrenata jactabit audacia? nihilne te nocturnum præsidium palatii, nihil urbis vigilæ, nihil timor populi, nihil consensus bonorum omnium, nihil hic munitissimus habendi senatus locus, nihil horum ora vultusque moverunt? patere tua consilia non sentis? constrictam jam omnium horum conscientia teneri conjurationem tuam non vides? quid proxima, quid superiore nocte egeris, ubi fueris, qous convocaveris, quid consilii ceperis, quem nostrum ignorare arbitraris? O tempora, o mores! Senatus hoc intelligit, consul videt: hic tamen vivit. Vivit? imo vero etiam in senatum venit: fit publici
ABCDEFGHIJKLMNOPQRSTUVWXYZ
ABCDEFGHIJKLMNOPQRSTUVWXYZŒÆ
1234567890

Quousque tandem abutere, Catilina, patientia nostra? quamdiu nos etiam furor iste tuus eludet? quem ad finem sese effrenata jactabit audacia? nihilne te nocturnum præsidium palatii, nihil urbis vigiliæ, nihil timor populi, nihil consensus bonorum omnium, nihil hic munitissimus habendi senatus locus, nihil horum ora vultusque moverunt? patere tua consilia non sentis? constrictam jam omnium horum conscientia teneri conjurationem tuam non vides? quid proxima, quid superiore nocte egeris, ubi fueris, quos convocaveris, quid consilii ceperis, quem nostrum ignorare arbitraris? O tempora, o mores! Senatus hoc intelligit, consul videt: hic tamen vivit. Vivit? imo vero etiam in senatum venit: fit publici consilii particeps: notat et designat oculis ad cædem unumquemque nostrum. Nos autem viri fortes satisfacere reipublicæ, videmur, si
ABCDEFGHIJKLMNOPQRSTUV WXYZ ÆŒ

E. White.   New-York

Plate 15 – Elihu White, 1817

contained a full showing of type as well as 118 ornaments[20] (Plates 16, 17). His previous training in business maneuvers gave him the experience to meet the competition springing up around him. He lowered prices (44 cents for pica, 56 cents for long primer, 76 cents for brevier); he extended credit— "for approved Notes, or acceptances at six months, payable in New-York, or at a liberal discount for cash."[21] This comprehensive specimen displays the modern faces which were favored by the printers of that time. Judged by the standards of those printers, the specimen is impressive, exemplifying White's success. This is verified by Bruce's comment that White, despite his interest in mechanical typefounding, did not "neglect attention to a correct style of faces, and had many that were highly prized."[22]

In his later years White's obsession with a typefounding machine revived. It needed merely the persuasion of William M. Johnson that his plans were feasible and should be sponsored.[23] The machines which White and Johnson produced, however, did not work efficiently enough to provide a satisfactory profit. Therefore, no other founder purchased them, although White himself was using them in his foundries at the time of his death in New York on November 7, 1836.[24] After his death the

[20] A Specimen of Printing Types from the Foundry of E. White (New York, 1821). Copy in NNC-Typ.

[21] Ibid., p. 2.

[22] David Bruce, [Jr.], "Type-founding in the United States," Typographic Messenger, III (Jan. 1868), p. 17.

[23] Bruce, Typ. Mess., III (Nov. 1867), 2.

[24] Bruce, Typ. Mess., III (Jan. 1868), p. 17; New York Evening Post, Nov. 8, 1836.

firm continued under the direction of his descendants until it was succeeded by Farmer, Little & Co. in 1862.

White's proclivity for mechanics also enabled him to obtain what MacKellar called "the means of multiplying matrices with facility."[25] As soon as his New York business was firmly entrenched he started to establish branch foundries in other cities. His foundries in Boston and Cincinnati had been the first in each city. They began as agencies of the New York firm, but White did not retain ownership of one for very long. Instead, for reasons unknown, he soon sold the Boston foundry to members of the local book trade.

The Boston foundry opened in 1817 and the New York specimen book of that year offered:

The following sizes exhibited in this specimen, may be had at the Charlestown Foundry, by applying to D. Manly, viz.

Double Pica,	Long Primer No 4.
Great Primer,	Burgeois No. 2.
Pica No. 3.	Brevier No. 2.
Small Pica No. 4.	Minion No. 2, and 3.

Orders left with said Manly for any of the other sizes, will be forwarded from New-York without delay.[26]

Boston printers could now obtain type locally at New York prices, certainly a welcome convenience.[27] At the beginning, David Manly employed

[25] Thomas MacKellar, *The American Printer* (Philadelphia, 1893), p. 22.
[26] *A Specimen ... of E. White* (1817), p. 2.
[27] *Ibid.*

Pica, on Small Pica Body.

Quousque tandem abutere, Catilina, patientia nostra?
quamdiu nos etiam furor iste tuus eludet? quem ad finem
sese effrenata jactabit audacia? nihilne te nocturnum præ-
sidiium palatii, nihil urbis vigiliæ, nihil timor populi, nihil
consensus bonorum omnium, nihil hic munitissimus haben
di senatus locus, nihil horum ora vultusque moverunt? patere tua consilia non sentis? constrictam jam omnium horum conscientia teneri conjurationem tuam non vides?
quid proxima, quid superiore nocte egeris, ubi fueris, quos
convocaveris, quid consilii ceperis, quem nostrum ignorare arbitraris? O tempora, o mores! Senatus hoc intelligit,
consul videt: hic tamen vivit. Vivit? imo vero etiam in senatum venit: fit publici consilii particeps: notat et designat oculis ad cædem unumquemque nostrum. Nos autem
viri fortes satisfacere reipublicæ videmur, si istius furorem
ac tela vitemus. Ad mortem te, Catilina, duci jussu consulis jam pridem oportebat: in te conferri pestem istam,
quam in tu nos omnes jamdiu machinaris. An vero vir
ABCDEFGHIJKLMNOPQRSTVUWXYZ ÆŒ
1234567890

Quosque tandem abutere, Catalina, patientia nostra? quam-
diu nos etiam furor iste tuus eludet? quem ad finem sese
effrenata jactabit audacia? nihilne te nocturnum præsidium
palatii, nihil urbis vigiliæ, nihil timor populi, nihil consen-
sus bonorum omnium, nihil hic munitissimus habendi sena-
tus locas, nihil horum ora vultusque moverunt? patere tua
consilia non sentis? constrictam jam omnium horum consci-
entia teneri conjurationem tuam non vides? quid proxima,
quid superiore nocte egeris, ubi fueris, quos convocaveris,
quid consilii ceperis, quem nostrum ignorare arbitraris? O
tempora, o mores! Senatus hoc intelligit, consul videt: hic
hic tamen vivit. Vivit? imo vero etiam in senatum venit: fit
publici consilii particeps: notat et designat oculis ad cædem
unumquemque nostrum. Nos autem viri fortes satisfacere
reipublicæ videmur, si istius furorem ac tela vitemus. Ad
mortem te, Catilini, duci jussu consulis jam pridem oporte-
bat: in te conferri pestem istam, quam tu in nos omnes jam-
diu machinaris. An vero vir amplissimus P. Scipio pon-
ABCDEFGHIJKLMNOPQRSTVUWXYZ

Plate 16 – Elihu White, 1821

DOUBLE PICA BLACK.

And be it further hereby enacted, That the Mayors, Bailiffs, or other Officer

PICA BLACK.

And be it further hereby enacted, That the Mayors, Bailiffs, or other he ad Officers of every Town and place corporate, and City within this Com monwealth, being Justice or Justices of Peace, shall have the same aut=

LONG PRIMER BLACK.

And be it further hereby enacted, That the Mayors, Bailiffs, or other head Officers of every Town and place corporate, and City within this Commonwealth, being Justice or Justices of Peace, shall have the same authority by virtue of this Act, within the limits and precincts of their Jurisdictions, as well out of Sessions, as at their Sessions, if they hold any, as is herein limited, prescribed, and

TWO LINES NONPAREIL MERIDIAN SHADE.

ABCDEFGHIJKLMNOPQRSTUVWXYZ &$.,-?!!! 1234567890

Plate 17 — Elihu White, 1821

two casters, but at the year's end the foundry left Charlestown for more space offered at the rear of Armstrong's Book Store, 50 Cornhill, Boston.[28]

When apparently all was going well, White decided to sell out; on May 19, 1819, the *Columbian Centinel* announced that Timothy Bedlington and Charles Ewer had purchased the Boston Type Foundry from E. White. Evidently Bedlington, a bookbinder, and Ewer, a bookseller, regarded this as an investment. Since neither wished to direct it, they engaged a typefounder, Edward Haskell, as manager. Under Haskell three young employees— Edward Pelouze, Sewell Phelps, Michael Dalton— learned the craft in which they achieved noteworthy reputations.[29] Ewer probably maintained the surveillance; orders for type were received at his bookstore.[30] In 1820 Bedlington and Ewer produced *A Specimen of Printing Types Cast at the Boston Foundry*, thereby demonstrating that they could supply a complete assortment of sizes as well as flowers and signs (Plate 18).

Two years later Timothy H. Carter, manager of the Boston bookstore of Cummings & Hilliard, bought the foundry and immediately proceeded to invest capital to increase the volume.[31] Carter trans-

[28] "History of the Boston Type Foundry," *Printer's Bull.*, June 1867, p. 1; *Columbian Centinel*, May 3, 1817; June 3, 1818.

[29] Steve L. Watts, "The Pelouze Family of Typefounders," *PaGA*, IV (1956), 31; "Hist. Boston Type Foundry," p. 1.

[30] *A Specimen of Printing Types Cast at the Boston Foundry* ([Boston], 1820), p. 1. Copy in MB.

[31] "Hist. Boston Type Foundry," p. 1.

acted this business with the zest which was later to make him a pre-eminent American publisher. He put his brother Charles in charge and moved the foundry to a building which he had erected in Harvard Place.[32] Then he arranged for Jedidiah Howe to bring stereotyping apparatus from New York, set it in place, and stay for a few days to teach a member of the staff, Lyman Thurston.[33] Thus Carter started the first stereotype foundry in Boston. James Conner, from the shop of John Watts, one of the first stereotypers in America, arrived to supervise its finishing department; he later returned to New York to become a major typefounder.[34]

In 1823 the foundry moved to Salem Street and larger quarters next to the church made famous by Paul Revere (Plate 19).[35] The next year, Charles C. Little, later of Little, Brown & Co., was admitted to partnership.[36] The official firm name was T. Harrington Carter & Co. at that time, although it also called itself the Boston Type and Stereotype Foundry. After so much good fortune in consolidation, a fire on June 23, 1824, interrupted business for three months.[37] When production resumed the firm issued a *Specimen of Modern Printing Types and Stereotype Cuts* (Plates 20, 21). The prefa-

[32] T. H. Carter, *A Brief Autobiographical Sketch* (n.p., 1888), p. 4.
[33] "Hist. Boston Type Foundry," p. 1.
[34] *Am. Dict. Print.*, p. 113; "Hist. Boston Type Foundry," p. 1.
[35] "Hist. Boston Type Foundry," p. 1.
[36] *Columbian Centinel*, Feb. 7, 1824.
[37] Boston *Daily Advertiser*, June 25, 1824; *Columbian Centinel*, Oct. 6, 1824.

Quousque tandem abutere, Catilina, patientia nostra? quamdiu nos etiam furor iste tuus eludet? quem ad finem sese effrenata jactabit audacia? nihilne te nocturnum præsidium palatii, nihil urbis vigiliæ, nihil timor populi, nihil consensus bonorum omnium, nihil hic munitissimus habendi senatus locus, nihil horum ora vultusque moverunt? patere tua consilia non sentis? constrictam jam omnium horum conscientia teneri conjurationem tuam non vides? quid proxima, quid superiore nocte egeris, ubi fueris, quos convocaveris, quid consilii ceperis, quem

ABCDEFGHIJKLMNOPQRSTUVWX
ABCDEFGHIJKLMNOPQRSTUVWXYZÆŒ.

Quousque tandem abutere, Catilina, patientia nostra? quamdiu nos etiam furor iste tuus eludet? quem ad finem sese effrenata jactabit audacia? nihilne te nocturnum præsidium palatii, nihil urbis vigiliæ, nihil timor populi, nihil consensus bonorum omnium, nihil hic munitissimus habendi senatus locus, nihil horum ora vultusque moverunt? patere tua consilia non sentis? constrictam jam omnium horum conscientia teneri conjurationem tuam non vides? quid proxima, quid superiore nocte egeris, ubi fueris, quos convocaveris,

ABCDEFGHIJKLMNOPQRSTUVW
$1234567890.

Plate 18 — Boston Foundry, 1820

Plate 19 – The Boston Type Foundry in 1823, near the historic Christ Church, in Salem Street, Boston. (From *Specimens from the Boston Type Foundry*, Boston, 1883)

tory note, dated January 1825, shows an aesthetic concern with form and an overall integrity:

T. H. Carter & Co. respectfully submit to the Printers of the United States, the following Specimen of Modern Printing Types, which is but a partial one of their Foundry, being their intention to issue one more complete, the ensuing season. Since the loss of their Foundry by fire in June last, they have with incessant activity and great expense, provided themselves with New Letter, *equal*, certainly, to any cast in this country: well adapted, they believe, to the critical taste of the present day.—In addition to the Types exhibited in this Specimen, they have five New Founts now *fitting up*, in which it has been their aim to combine the beauty of the Modern Style with the clearness and durability of the Scotch Type; they have also in a state of forwardness, Founts of Greek and German, and a variety of Large and Ornamental Letter, Flowers, Cuts, &c. and are constantly making additions to their Foundry.

They have at all times on hand, almost every article which Printers use; as, Brass Rule, Type Cases, Composing Sticks, Demi and Royal Chases, Press Boards, Case Stands, Ball Skins, Ball Stocks, Parchment, Printing Ink of every quality and price, a great variety of Ornamental Letter Cuts, &c. and receive orders for Ramage, Rust, and Wells' Printing Presses. They have generally on hand, Types which have been once used for Stereotyping, but little worn, subject to discounts of from 10 to 20 per cent. Every article furnished by them they warrant to be good, and their terms are as liberal as those of other Foundries. They can assure their Customers and Printers generally, that they have experienced and skilful workmen, and that in the

Composition of the Metal and Manufacturing of
their Types, the greatest attention and care is given:
and having every facility for executing orders with
correctness and despatch, they hope to merit a con-
tinuance of the patronage they have so liberally received. They will also furnish Types for their customers from the other Foundries, if desired.[38]

The modern face was decidedly holding its own
despite some misgivings about its clarity. Many, if
not all, of the punches may have been cut by Edward
Pelouze who, having begun his career with Bedlington & Ewer, grew along with the firm to become
"one of the best punch cutters of his time."[39] Within
the short period of three years the Carters converted
a small foundry into a large and busy printers' warehouse. They built so well that their prestige was one
of the resources of the Boston Type and Stereotype
Foundry which survived until it was absorbed into
the American Type Founders Company in 1892.

Elihu White was caught up in the fervor of western expansion, as was to be expected of a man who
loved to be on the move. Two years after establishing the first Boston typefoundry he chose Cincinnati, the most advantageous western settlement, as
the site for an agency, envisioning in its spurt of
population growth the development of a printing
trade of major significance. He selected one of his
most skilled employees, Oliver Wells, to be foundry
manager. Wells, originally a clockmaker, had been
trained by White during the early Hartford days

[38] *Specimen of Modern Printing Types and Stereotype
Cuts* (Boston, 1825), pp. 3–4. Copy in NNC-Typ.
[39] Watts, "The Pelouze Family," p. 31.

Quousque tandem abutere, Catilina, patientia nostra? quamdiu nos etiam furor iste tuus eludet? quem ad finem sese effrenata jactabit audacia? nihilne te nocturnum præsidium palatii, nihil urbis vigiliæ, nihil timor populi, nihil consensus bonorum omnium, nihil hic munitissimus habendi senatus locus, nihil horum ora vultusque moverunt? patere tua consilia non sentis? constrictam jam omnium horum conscientia teneri conjurationem tuam non
ABCDEFGHIJKLMNOPQRSTUVWXYZÆ
ABCDEFGHIJKLMNOPQRSTUVWXYZÆŒ
£ 1234567890. ¹¹¹¹²³³⁵⁷/₂₃₄₈₃₄₈₈₈ $

Quousque tandem abutere, Catilina, patientia nostra? quamdiu nos etiam furor iste tuus eludet? quem ad finem sese effrenata jactabit audacia? nihilne te nocturnum præsidium palatii, nihil urbis vigiliæ, nihil timor populi, nihil consensus bonorum omnium, nihil hic munitissimus habendi senatus locus, nihil horum ora vultusque moverunt? patere tua consilia non sentis? constrictam jam omnium horum conscientia teneri conjurationem tuam non
ABCDEFGHIJKLMNOPQRSTUVWXYZÆ

In the second century of the Christian Æra, the Empire of Rome comprehended the fairest part of the Earth, and the most civilized portion of mankind. The frontiers of that extensive monarchy were guarded by ancient renown and disciplined valour. The gentle, but powerful influence of laws and manners had gradually cemented the union of the provinces. Their peaceful inhabitants enjoyed and abused the advantages of wealth and luxury. The image of a free constitution was preserved with decent reverence.

T. H. CARTER & Co. BOSTON, 1825.

Plate 20

PICA BLACK.

We hold these truths to be self-evident: that all Men are created equal; that they are endowed by their Creator with certain unalienable rights; that among these are life, liberty, and the pursuit of happiness; that to secure these rights governments are instituted among men, deriving their just

ABCDEFGHIJKLMNOPQRSTUVWXYZ&

LONG PRIMER BLACK.

We hold these truths to be self-evident; that all Men are created equal; that they are endowed by their Creator with certain unalienable rights; that among these are life, liberty, and the pursuit of happiness; that to secure these rights governments are instituted among men, deriving their just powers from the consent of the governed; that whenever any form of government becomes destructive of these ends, it is the right of the people to alter or to abolish it, and to institute new government,

ABCDEFGHIJKLMNOPQRSTUVWXYZ&

TWO LINE BREVIER SHADED.

ABCDEFGHIJKLMNOPQRSTUVW
XYZÆŒ&.,;:?!'-

T. H. CARTER & Co. Boston, 1825.

Plate 21

and had followed him to New York.[40] His son Horace could build the cases, stands, and presses needed in the new territory, a fortuitous arrangement which, of course, White, adept at turning things to advantage, had probably planned when he selected Wells.[41] All preparations in order, the group left for Cincinnati where, with a patriotic flourish, they cast their first type on July 4, 1820.[42]

Carefully judging the provincialism of the new West, White appointed a Cincinnati bookseller, John P. Foote, as his business agent. Thus, as Sutton indicates, the branch known as the Cincinnati Type Foundry would be duly regarded by Westerners as an indigenous enterprise, and it would be assumed that the money received would stay in the West.[43] Under these auspices the foundry was eagerly welcomed by the community and Sutton quotes from a responsive article written when the foundry was about to open:

The delay, inconvenience, and expense of procuring printing types from New York or Philadelphia, operate as serious discouragements; these will be completely overcome as soon as this foundry shall be in full operation. It will moreover prove a considerable saving to us, as the money that would otherwise be sent across the mountains for these articles will now be retained at home.[44]

[40] *Am. Dict. Print.*, p. 580.
[41] *Typographic Messenger*, II (July 1867), 65.
[42] *Ibid.*
[43] Walter Sutton, *The Western Book Trade* (Columbus, 1961), p. 13.
[44] *Ibid.*

In Cincinnati, as in Boston, White offered "supplies at eastern prices."[45] As a consequence of putting Horace Wells in charge of wooden equipment, the Cincinnati Type Foundry and Printers' Warehouse steadily increased the number of items for sale until "his industry soon produced a surplus stock."[46] There seemed to be no limit to his ingenuity for in time he worked in iron in addition to type-dressing and punchcutting.[47] The elder Wells conducted the foundry successfully, becoming a partner in 1823 when the firm name was changed to Foote & Wells.[48] Father and son advanced themselves still further when Foote withdrew in 1825; they took charge with Nathan Guilford, Foote's successor in the book business, as silent partner.[49] A respectful account of the foundry written by Drake and Mansfield appeared in 1826:

The Messrs. Wells' Type Foundry and Printers' Warehouse, is situated on Walnut street, between Third and Fourth, where they manufacture, in a superior manner, all kinds of type, presses, chases, composing sticks, proof gallies, brass rule, &c. &c. at the eastern prices. They employ about 23 hands. This valuable establishment has entirely superseded the importation of type and other printing materials from the eastern states.[50]

Elihu White held his interest in the firm until the 1830s.[51] He had extended his craft northward and

[45] *Ibid.*, p. 14.   [46] *Typ. Mess.*, II (July 1867), 65.
[47] *Ibid.*   [48] Sutton, *West. Book Trade*, p. 13.
[49] *Ibid.*   [50] *Ibid.*, p. 14.
[51] *Typ. Mess.*, II (July 1867), 66.

westward. His crowded life had been committed to one end—the advancement and spread of typefounding in a pioneering nation. To White, the son-in-law of the author of *McFingal*, his own exciting and romantic adventure must have been worthwhile despite the memories of inventions that came to nothing, the promotions and intrigues that must have failed, and the heartbreak that often underlies even the most glorious business career.[52] The Cincinnati foundry, too, continued until it became part of the American Type Founders Company in 1892.

About 1812 Edwin Starr with his brothers, Richard and James Fosdick, opened a foundry in New York in competition with White, but their small capital was soon swallowed up by war and inflation.[53] Simultaneously two New York printers, David and George Bruce, were struggling with the problem of finding type of the proper shape for their stereotyping facilities. Available type had no shoulder; the beard sloped at a long angle from face to shank, and the plaster used in stereotyping filled the space made by the angles. Since founders feared that stereotyping would reduce sales, they could not be persuaded to make type with square shoulders. The Bruces decided to make their own type as a way out of their troubles and, furnishing capital to the Starr brothers, they formed the partnership of Bruce & Starr. The firm, so listed in the 1814 New

[52] Thompson R. Harlow, in a letter dated Dec. 10, 1962, states that Elihu White married Sarah Trumbull (*Courant*, March 9, 1808) who died in New York June 10, 1816 (*Courant*, June 18, 1816).

[53] Bruce, *Typ. Mess.*, III (Nov. 1867), 2.

York directory, ended within a year, the Starrs selling their remaining interest to the Bruces.[54]

By 1816 two more Starr brothers were in the book trade. Henry, trained as a printer, worked in Philadelphia as early as 1813; Charles arrived in New York in 1815, becoming a stereotype founder.[55] The later careers of all five brothers deserve mention. Henry turned to engraving and letter-cutting; James Fosdick was a stereotyper in New York, Boston, Philadelphia, and Baltimore; Charles became contractor and superintendent of the binding department of the American Bible Society as well as a founder of both the American Tract Society and New York University.[56] Edwin Starr, working at the Boston Type and Stereotype Foundry, patented (with John Sturdevant), a typecasting machine in 1827; he was, according to De Vinne, "a punch-cutter and inventor of ability."[57] De Vinne also states that in "partnership with his son Thomas W. he carried on the business of type-founding in Baltimore and Philadelphia under the name of E. Starr

    [54] "Mr. David Bruce," *Typographic Messenger*, II (March 1867), 34.

    [55] Brown and Brown, *Direct. of the Book-Arts*, p. 113; George L. McKay, *A Register of Artists, Engravers, Booksellers, Bookbinders, Printers & Publishers in New York City, 1633–1820* (New York, 1942), p. 68; Burgis Pratt Starr, *A History of the Starr Family* (Hartford, 1879), p. 196; *American Bibliography . . . for 1816*, comp. Ralph R. Shaw and Richard H. Shoemaker (New York, 1963), p. 86.

    [56] Starr, *Hist. Starr Family*, pp. 189–96; De Vinne, *Pract. of Typ.*, p. 104.

    [57] Information in a communication from T. B. Morrow, U.S. Dept. of Commerce, March 12, 1954; De Vinne, *Pract. of Typ.*, p. 104.

& Son."[58] In 1853 E. Starr & Son became Collins & McLeester, which firm remained in business until it became part of the American Type Founders Company in 1892.[59]

Richard Starr apparently moved to Philadelphia about 1813.[60] Within five years he and John M. Reich had organized Reich, Starr & Co., stereotype and letter founders. A prefatory note dated April 1, 1818, in their specimen book of that year discloses that the foundry lacked sufficient stock and money:

It must be readily perceived that a considerable time is required to prepare and finish a complete assortment; but we shall exert our utmost efforts to accomplish this object as speedily as possible: and, in the mean time, should types be wanted, of which we have not, as yet, prepared specimens, we can, and will, upon receiving orders, instantly commence the execution thereof and complete them without delay.
We find ourselves under the necessity of respectfully suggesting that, in the extent of our credit, *we cannot well exceed* four months; and of stating, that in preference *even to that* we would allow a discount of four per cent. for cash.... If, by an increase of patronage we should hereafter become enabled to extend our credits, we shall be found as liberal as any others in that respect, especially to such as, by their early support, shall contribute to the means of enabling us to become so.[61]

[58] De Vinne, *Pract. of Typ.*, p. 104.
[59] Information in a communication from Ralph Green, March 28, 1952.
[60] Brown and Brown, *Direct. of the Book-Arts*, p. 113.
[61] *Specimen of Printing Types by Reich, Starr & Co.* (Philadelphia, 1818), p. 1. Copy in NNC-Typ.

The showing included three long primer (one condensed) and a brevier as well as a brevier on minion (Plate 22). Joel Munsell characterized Reich-Starr type as "highly extolled"; and stated that it "is particularly mentioned that their English backslope was a beautiful specimen of fancy letter."[62] Although they furnished good type, they could not break into the Philadelphia market. About 1826 Richard Starr opened a typefoundry in Albany. A circular letter of the Albany Type Foundry, Richard Starr & Co., dated October 20, 1826, asserts that "one of this concern has been engaged in letter-cutting for more than fifteen years," and that "he has cut more than one-half of all the letter now cast by all the American Founders."[63] Some day, it is hoped, the contribution of the five Starr brothers will be comprehensively investigated.

No matter what else the Starrs accomplished for typefounding, they should be remembered as the agents through whom the Bruces entered the craft. Both Bruce brothers had been printers. David, the elder, born in Wick, Scotland, November 12, 1770, was probably raised in Edinburgh, where his parents had fled to escape their evil laird. At an early age he went to sea: "Before the age of nineteen, he had been scorched by the tropical suns of the East and West Indies; had shivered in the icy gales of the Greenland fisheries; and had served a short term, through impressment, in H. B. M. Channel Fleet,

[62] Munsell, *Typ. Misc.*, p. 135.
[63] De Vinne, *Pract. of Typ.*, p. 104.

Pica, No. 1.

Quousque tandem abutere, Catilina, patientia nostra? quamdiu nos etiam furor iste tuus eludet? quem ad finem sese effrenata jactabit audacia? nihilne te nocturnum præsidium palatii, nihil urbis vigiliæ, nihil timor populi, nihil consensus bonorum omnium, nihil hic munitissimus habendi senatus locus, nihil horum ora vultusque moverunt? patere tua consilia non sentis? constrictam jam omnium horum conscientia teneri conjurationem tuam non vides? quid proxima, quid superiore nocte egeris, ubi fueris, quos convocaveris, quid consilii ceperis, quem nostrum ignorare arbitraris? O tempora, o mores! Senatus hoc intelligit, consul vidit: hic tamen vivit. Vivit? imo vero etiam in senatum venit: fit publici consilii particeps: notat et designat oculis ad cædem unumquemque nos-

ABCDEFGHIJKLMNOPQRSTUVWXYZ

ABCDEFGHIJKLMNOPQRSTUVWXYZÆŒ

1234567890 $

Quousque tandem abutere, Catilina, patientia nostra? quamdiu nos etiam furor iste tuus eludet? quem ad finem sese effrenata jactabit audacia? nihilne te nocturnum præsidium palatii, nihil urbis vigiliæ, nihil timor populi, nihil consensus bonorum omnium, nihil hic munitissimus habendi senatus locus, nihil horum ora vultusque moverunt? patere tua consilia non sentis? constrictam jam omnium horum conscientia teneri conjurationem tuam non vides? quid proxima, quid superiore nocte egeris, ubi fueris, quos convocaveris, quid consilii ceperis, quem nostrum ignorare arbitraris? O tempora, o mores! Senatus hoc intelligit, consul vidit: hic tamen vivit. Vivit? imo vero etiam in senatum venit: fit publici consilii particeps: notat et designat oculis

ABCDEFGHIJKLMNOPRSTUVWXYZ

Plate 22 — Reich, Starr & Co., 1818

under Admiral Howe."[64] Following his discharge
he served an apprenticeship in the King's printing
office, Edinburgh. His humble prospects set him to
dreaming about the magical opportunities in America and he emigrated to New York, arriving in the
spring of 1793.[65] Immediately he found a job as
pressman on a daily newspaper; he remained about
a year, thereafter moving to Philadelphia where he
was employed by Hall & Sellers.[66] His happiness
with the personal freedom which Americans enjoyed persuaded him to send for his younger brother
George before the boy could be drafted for military
service. His family in Edinburgh had already lost
one son in the Napoleonic wars and willingly agreed
to the proposal.[67]

George arrived in Philadelphia, unaccompanied,
on his fourteenth birthday, June 26, 1795.[68] He
learned to print in the shop of Thomas Dobson and
then, after two years, worked for the Philadelphia
Gazette.[69] The two brothers respected their craft
and learned all they could, studying even after the
usual long working day. In Philadelphia David cul-
tivated the friendship of Archibald Binny, a former

[64] "Mr. David Bruce," *Typ. Mess.*, II (March 1867),
33.
[65] *Ibid.*   [66] *Ibid.; Am. Dict. Print.*, p. 73.
[67] "Mr. David Bruce," *Typ. Mess.*, II (March 1867),
33; Lyman Horace Weeks, *Book of Bruce* (New York,
[1907]), pp. 321–22.
[68] "Mr. George Bruce," *Typographic Messenger*, I
(Sept. 1866), 81; Weeks, *Book of Bruce*, p. 321.
[69] "Mr. George Bruce," *Typ. Mess.*, I (Sept. 1866), 81;
Weeks, *Book of Bruce*, p. 322.

fellow-member of the Edinburgh radical club, and sought out members of the Friends of the People, as well as Adam Ramage, the pressmaker, and James Ronaldson. As one biographer has said, "Any matters pertaining to the perfection of the Art of Printing received their warmest attention."[70]

A yellow fever epidemic in the city disrupted the congenial and rewarding association with their countrymen. To escape the sickness they fled to the north, but on the way George fell ill and was nursed back to health by his elder brother. They reached New York, then went to Albany, both working in the office of the *Centinel* in 1798.[71] The following year they returned to New York, George continuing as printer there and David sometimes "itinerating as a journeyman in the principal cities, but most generally locating in either New York or Philadelphia."[72] During this period David opened a printing ink plant which soon failed for lack of capital.[73] In 1803 George became printer of the New York *Daily Advertiser*.[74] But the minds of these two indefatigable young men were focused on one ambition, the ownership of a printing business, toward which they persevered until, about the end of 1805, they hired press and type, rented the rooms formerly used by James Rivington, and started composing the first

[70] "Mr. David Bruce," *Typ. Mess.*, II (March 1867), 33.
[71] Weeks, *Book of Bruce*, p. 322.
[72] *Ibid.;* "Mr. David Bruce," *Typ. Mess.*, II (March 1867), 33.
[73] McKay, *Register*, p. 14; "Mr. David Bruce," *Typ. Mess.*, II (March 1867), 33.
[74] Weeks, *Book of Bruce*, p. 323.

book printed by the firm of D. & G. Bruce, Lavoisier's *Elements of Chemistry* (1806).[75]

In their effort to produce work of quality, they were the first printers in New York to press the sheets themselves rather than leave this task to the binder. For this, "they received severe denunciation from the craft for making what was deemed an unwarrantable innovation upon the established order of things in printing offices."[76] The results of a concentration on good work at competitive prices came quickly: the volume of trade increased until within three years they moved to Slote Lane, setting up their nine Ramage presses in the largest printing office in New York.[77] That the Bruces could manage such an organization may be explained by a providential combination of their personal traits, a balance of audacity and discretion:

There was a most remarkable similitude in the mental and moral forces of the brothers Bruce, which made them peculiarly fitted for each other, and for success, which it is doubtful if separately applied might not have been so prosperous. Industry, perseverance, tact, and moral stamina, with a dash of what is termed genius, were equally their endowments; but here the similitude must cease. David, the elder, was as much noted for his impetuosity, and inflammatory outbreaks of temper, as was his brother for that of coolness, self-control, and self-possession.[78]

[75] "Mr. David Bruce," *Typ. Mess.*, II (March 1867), 33; Weeks, *Book of Bruce*, p. 323.
[76] "Mr. David Bruce," *Typ. Mess.*, II (March 1867), 33.
[77] "Mr. George Bruce," *Typ. Mess.*, I (Sept. 1866), 81.
[78] *Ibid.*

As news of the development of stereotyping trickled into New York, David Bruce, realizing the potentialities of the invention and hoping to learn all about the new art, obtained letters of introduction to the Earl of Stanhope. He sailed to England in 1812 to find the Earl courteous in his refusal to tell him much about stereotyping. Bruce, as usual undismayed, managed somehow to search out facts on the process of molding. He returned home to experiment, trying one idea after another until he had workable results; in the meantime he devised the very important planing machine, the mahogany shifting blocks, as well as a method of packing plates in boxes. This was the time when he judged it necessary, as he could not get type with the proper shape for stereotyping, to enter the typefounding business. The firm of Bruce & Starr soon became D. & G. Bruce, Letter-founders, 27 William Street.

As soon as the Bruces estimated that they had mastered the art of stereotyping, they decided to attempt an edition of the Bible. A series of letters to Mathew Carey, which are now in the Historical Society of Pennsylvania, discloses their cautious approach to this new business. They began by offering to sell duplicate plates outside of New York City:

New York, April 9, 1814

Sir

We are now Stereotyping the octavo Bible, as per specimen page, and expect to complete it in the course of the year. We wish to sell a set of the plates in Philadelphia, and offer it to you in the first instance. The Old and New Testament and Apocrapha will be comprised in 1128 pages, the plates of which we will sell at $3.50 each, making a total of $3948. We propose to deliver it in five parts of about 224 plates. Each delivery to be paid for in a note at 90 days. The cost of these plates is only about one third of what it would cost to get the same work up with common types, and they will last much longer.

We are sir
your obt. servts
D & G BRUCE

Mr M. Carey.[79]

This proposal for a comparatively inexpensive yet durable standing Bible was attractive to Mathew Carey, "the foremost printer and publisher of the Bible in America" at that time.[80] Carey apparently did not question the claim to durability, for he was anxious for a Testament as soon as possible, other works to be delivered later. The concluding sentence of the Bruce reply to Carey affirms that they were unaware of the possibilities of the process:[81]

New York, April 15, 1814.

Sir

Your favour of the 13th is received. We have the Testament in hand, and would sell a set of the plates at $2.25 per page, amounting to $756 for the

[79] The Bruce-Carey correspondence is printed with the kind permission of the Historical Society of Pennsylvania.

[80] Hills, *English Bible*, p. 15.

[81] Cf. "They conceived the idea of adding the then new business of Stereotyping as an adjunct, mainly for the purpose of publishing their own works" ("Mr. George Bruce," *Typ. Mess.*, I [Sept. 1866], 81).

whole. We would allow $25 per cwt. for your old Testament on account, if you would deliver it immediately, as the value of metal must fall soon. Our Testament will be completed in July.

We have no scale of prices for stereotyping and dont intend to make a general business of it.

We are Sir

your obt. servts

D & G BRUCE

Mr M. Carey

This was satisfactory to Carey, but he had a few questions which were answered by the Bruces:

New York, April 27, 1814

Sir

Your favour of yesterday is received. We think our Testament will be completed by the 10th of July, but cannot say that we are absolutely certain of it. It will make fourteen sheets. We copy from the Edinburgh edition, which is page for page with the New York, but more correct.

We shall use mahogany blocks, worth two dollars a piece, as is now the general practice in London. They may be surrounded by four pieces of wood, and quoined up at the corner-irons of the press, the same as in a chase, and need not be unlocked until the edition of the work is completed.

Your obt. servts

D & G BRUCE

Mr M. Carey

Carey then accepted the terms and on April 30, 1814, the Bruces acknowledged the order. But they found, to their cost, that they had been overoptimistic about the completion date.

On October 18 they wrote that the "plates of the Testament are all cast; they are now undergoing a

Quousque tandem abutere, Catilina, patientia nostra? quamdiu nos etiam furor iste tuus eludet? quem ad finem sese effrenata jactabit audacia? nihilne te nocturnum præsidium palatii, nihil urbis vigiliæ, nihil timor populi, nihil consensus bonorum omnium, nihil hic munitissimus habendi senatus locus, nihil horum ora vultusque moverunt? patere tua consilia non sentis? constrictam jam omnium horum conscientia teneri conjurationem tuam non vides? quid proxima, quid superiore nocte egeris, ubi fueris, quos convocaveris, quid consilii ceperis, quem nostrum ignorare arbitraris? O tempora, o mores! Senatus hoc intelligit, consul videt: hic tamen vivit. Vivit? imo vero etiam in senatum venit: fit publici consilii parti-

ABCDEFGHIJKLMNOPQRSTUVWXYZÆ

ABCDEFGHIJKLMNOPQRSTUVWXYZÆŒ

$ 1234567890 £

Quousque tandem abutere, Catilina, patientia nostra? quamdiu nos etiam furor iste tuus eludet? quem ad finem sese effrenata jactabit audacia? nihilne te nocturnum præsidium palatii, nihil urbis vigiliæ, nihil timor populi, nihil consensus bonorum omnium, nihil hic munitissimus habendi senatus locus, nihil horum ora vultusque moverunt? patere tua consilia non sentis? constrictam jam omnium horum conscientia teneri conjurationem tuam non vides? quid proxima, quid superiore nocte egeris ubi fueris quos convocaveris, quid consilii ceperis, quem nostrum ignorare arbitraris? O tempora, o mores! Senatus hoc intelligit, consul videt: hic tamen vivit. Vivit? imo vero etiam in senatum venit: fit publici consilii particeps: notat et designat oculis ad cædem unum-

ABCDEFGHIJKLMNOPQRSTUVWXYZÆ

D. & G. BRUCE, Letter-founders, No. 27 William-street, New-York. JUNE, 1815.

Plate 23

Quousque tandem abutere, Catilina, patientia nostra? quamdiu nos etiam furor iste tuus eludet? quem ad finem sese effrenata jactabit audacia? nihilne te nocturnum præsidium palatii, nihil urbis vigiliæ, nihil timor populi, nihil consensus bonorum omnium, nihil hic munitissimus habendi senatus locus, nihil horum ora vultusque moverunt? patere tua consilia non sentis? constrictam jam omnium horum conscientia teneri conjurationem tuam non vides? quid proxima, quid superiore nocte egeris, ubi fueris, quos convocaveris, quid consilii ceperis, quem nostrum ignorare arbitraris? O tempora, o mores! Senatus hoc intelligit, consul videt: hic tamen vivit. Vivit? imo vero etiam in senatum venit: fit publici consilii particeps: notat et designat oculis ad cædem unumquemque nostrum. Nos autem viri fortes satisfacere reipublicæ videmur, si istius furorem ac tela vitemus. Ad mortem te, Catilina, duci jussu consulis jam pridem oportebat: in te conferri pestem istam, quam tu in nos omnes jamdiu machinaris. An vero vir amplissimus P. Scipio pontifex maximus, Tiberium Gracchum mediocriter labefactantem statum reipublicæ privatis interfe-

ABCDEFGHIJKLMNOPQRSTUVWXYZÆŒ

ABCDEFGHIJKLMNOPQRSTUVWXYZÆŒ

1234567890

Quousque tandem abutere, Catilina, patientia nostra? quamdiu nos etiam furor iste tuus eludet? quem ad finem sese effrenata jactabit audacia? nihilne te nocturnum præsidium palatii, nihil urbis vigiliæ, nihil timor populi, nihil consensus bonorum omnium, nihil hic munitissimus habendi senatus locus, nihil horum ora vultusque moverunt? patere tua consilia non sentis? constrictam jam omnium horum conscientia teneri conjurationem tuam non vides? quid proxima, quid superiore nocte egeris, ubi fueris, quos convocaveris, quid consilii ceperis, quem nostrum ignorare arbitraris? O tempora, o mores! Senatus hoc intelligit, consul videt: hic tamen vivit. Vivit? imo vero etiam in senatum venit: fit publici consilii particeps: notat et designat oculis ad cædem unumquemque nostrum. Nos autem viri fortes satisfacere reipublicæ videmur, si istius furorem ac tela vitemus. Ad mortem te, Catilina, duci jussu consulis jam pridem oportebat: in te conferri pestem istam, quam tu in nos omnes jamdiu machinaris. An vero vir amplissimus P. Scipio pontifex maximus, Tiberium Gracchum mediocriter labefactantem statum reipublicæ privatis interfecit: Catilinam vero orbem terræ cæde atque incendiis vas-

ABCDEFGHIJKLMNOPQRSTUVWXYZÆŒ

D. & G. BRUCE, Letter-founders,
No. 27 William-street, New-York.   JUNE, 1815.

Plate 24

revision, and will be forwarded in the course of a week." Ten days later they informed Carey of another delay: "We have been disappointed in our expectation of completing your plates. Our men are much out on military duty. We send you five sheets as per receipt, and hope to forward the remainder next week." It was not until November 7 that the last of the plates were shipped and billed:

336 plates of New Testament @ 2.25 $756.
Cr June 25. By 16 cwt. 3 qrs.
  14 lbs Metal @ 25   421.88
                                  $334.12

Despite these initial frustrations David Bruce, with his self-confidence and diligence geared to economic success, developed a lucrative trade in stereotyping.

As typefounders the Bruces did not issue a specimen book immediately. Instead they produced a series of dated specimen sheets beginning in June 1815 (Plates 23–28). The specimen of pearl, July 1815, apparently completed the first series which could then be bound. It bears this note:

An anxiety to exhibit a perfect series of Printing Types, for Book-work, has delayed the publication of this Specimen longer than was perhaps compatible with the interests of the establishment. Some minute blemishes have still been permitted to pass, which will however be corrected without delay. On the whole, it is hoped that the great expense, and two years of labour, bestowed on this foundry, will be thought to have been well applied.[82]

[82] "Pearl"—one of a series of specimen sheets issued by D. & G. Bruce, New York, 1815. Copy in NNC-Typ.

This series included two pica faces, two small pica, four long primer, two bourgeois, two brevier, and two nonpareil–a wide assortment necessitated by the lack of type acceptable for stereotyping as well as by the vanity of the Bruces.

In 1818 they issued another series of specimens which included two-line letters and, like White, they ran a series of specimens at the end of Van Winkle's *Printers' Guide*[83] (Plate 29). Two years later, their specimen book, continually enlarged, quite unexpectedly exhibited their sense of superiority to any other domestic founder (Plate 30). The high-flown "Advertisement," dated April 1820, disparaged the type of Binny & Ronaldson and puffed up the influence of the Bruces with an alarming petulance:

The Art of Printing has confessedly received a great improvement within the last twenty years, both in Europe and this country. It was the consequence of a refinement, peculiar to this age, which requires, in every production of human industry, a degree of excellence seldom attempted before, and rarely reached. The specimens of the European type-founders exhibit a striking improvement in the form of their types, which contributed much to the elegance of modern printing; but, in this country, the want of active competition prevented any material improvement in the form and finish of types until within a very few years; and even the attempts at improvement, in the foundry which principally supplied the United States, previous to 1812, were mostly so unfortunate as to have been since con-

[83] Van Winkle, *Printers' Guide*, pp. 263–84.

Quousque tandem abutere, Catilina, patientia nostra? quamdiu nos etiam furor iste tuus eludet? quem ad finem sese effrenata jactabit audacia? nihilne te nocturnum præsidium palatii, nihil urbis vigiliæ, nihil timor populi, nihil consensus bonorum omnium, nihil hic munitissimus habendi senatus locus, nihil horum ora vultusque moverunt? patere tua consilia non sentis? constrictam jam omnium horum conscientia teneri conjurationem tuam non vides? quid proxima, quid superiore nocte egeris, ubi fueris, quos convocaveris, quid consilii ceperis, quem nostrum ignorare arbitraris? O tempora, o mores! Senatus hoc intelligit, consul videt: hic tamen Vivit. Vivit? imo vero etiam in senatum venit: fit publici consilii particeps: notat et designat oculis ad cædem unumquemque nostrum. Nos autem viri fortes satisfacere reipublicæ, videmur si istius furorem ac tela vitemus. Ad mortem te, Catilina, duci jussu consulis jam pridem oportebat: in te conferri pestem istam, quam tu in nos omnes jamdiu machinaris. An vero vir amplissimus P. Scipio pontifex maximus, Tiberium Gracchum mediocriter labefactantem statum reipublicæ privatis interfe-

ABCDEFGHIJKLMNOPQRSTUVWXYZÆŒ

Quousque tandem abutere, Catilina, patientia nostra? quamdiu nos etiam furor iste tuus eludet? quem ad finem sese effrenata jactabit audacia? nihilne te nocturnum præsidium palatii, nihil urbis vigiliæ, nihil timor populi, nihil consensus bonorum omnium, nihil hic munitissimus habendi senatus locus, nihil horum ora vultusque moverunt? patere tua consilia non sentis? constrictam jam omnium horum conscientia teneri conjurationem tuam non vides? quid proxima, quid superiore nocte egeris, ubi fueris, quos convocaveris, quid consilii ceperis, quem nostrum ignorare arbitraris? O tempora, o mores! Senatus hoc intelligit, consul videt: hic tamen vivit. Vivit? imo vero etiam in senatum venit: fit publici consilii particeps: notat et designat oculis ad cædem unumquemque nostrum. Nos autem viri fortes satisfacere reipublicæ videmur, si istius furorem ac tela vitemus. Ad mortem te, Catilina, duci jussu consulis jam pridem oportebat: in te conferri pestem istam, quam tu in nos omnes jamdiu machinaris. An vero vir amplissimus P. Scipio pontifex maximus, Tiberium Gracchum mediocriter labefactantem statum reipublicæ privatis interfecit: Catilinam vero orbem terræ cæde atque incendiis vas-

ABCDEFGHIJKLMNOPQRSTUVWXYZÆŒ

D. &. G. BRUCE, Letter-founders,
No. 27 William-street, New-York.   JUNE, 1815.

Plate 25

Quousque tandem abutere, Catilina, patientia nostra? quamdiu nos etiam furor iste tuus eludet? quem ad finem sese effrenata jactabit audacia? nihilne te nocturnum præsidium palatii, nihil urbis vigiliæ, nihil timor populi, nihil consensus bonorum omnium, nihil hic munitissimus habendi senatus locus, nihil horum ora vultusque moverunt? patere tua consilia non sentis? constrictam jam omnium horum conscientia teneri conjurationem tuam non vides? quid proxima, quid superiore nocte egeris, ubi fueris, quos convocaveris, quid consilii ceperis, quem nostrum ignorare arbitraris? O tempora, o mores! Senatus hoc intelligit, consul videt: hic tamen vivit. Vivit? imo vero etiam in senatum venit: fit publici consilii particeps: notat et designat oculis ad cædem unumquemque nostrum. Nos autem viri fortes satisfacere reipublicæ videmur, si istius furorem ac tela vitemus. Ad mortem te, Catilina, duci jussu consulis jam pridem oportebat: in te conferri pestem istam, quam tu in nos omnes jamdiu machinaris. An vero vir amplissimus P. Scipio pontifex maximus, Tiberium Gracchum mediocriter labefactantem statum reipublicæ privatis interfecit: Catilinam vero orbem ter-

ABCDEFGHIJKLMNOPQRSTUVWXYZÆŒ
ABCDEFGHIJKLMNOPQRSTUVWXYZÆŒ
1234567890

Quousque tandem abutere, Catilina, patientia nostra? quamdiu nos etiam furor iste tuus eludet? quem ad finem sese effrenata jactabit audacia? nihilne te nocturnum præsidium palatii, nihil urbis vigiliæ, nihil timor populi, nihil consensus bonorum omnium, nihil hic munitissimus habendi senatus locus, nihil horum ora vultusque moverunt? patere tua consilia non sentis? constrictam jam omnium horum conscientia teneri conjurationem tuam non vides? quid proxima, quid superiore, nocte egeris, ubi fueris, quos convocaveris, quid consilii ceperis, quem nostrum ignorare arbitraris? O tempora, o mores! Senatus hoc intelligit, consul videt: hic tamen vivit. Vivit? imo vero etiam in senatum venit: fit publici consilii particeps: notat et designat oculis ad cædem unumquemque nostrum. Nos autem viri fortes satisfacere reipublicæ videmur, si istius furorem ac tela vitemus. Ad mortem te, Catilina, duci jussu consulis jam pridem oportebat: in te conferri pestem istam, quam tu in nos omnes jamdiu machinaris. An vero vir amplissimus, P. Scipio, pontifex maximus, Tiberium Gracchum mediocriter labefactantem statum reipublicæ privatus interfecit: Catilinam vero orbem terræ cæde atque incendiis vastare cupientem nos consules

ABCDEFGHIJKLMNOPQRSTUVWXYZÆŒ

D. & G. BRUCE, Letter-founders,
No. 27 William-street, New-York.   JUNE, 1815.

Plate 26

demned by the proprietors of that respectable establishment. In this state of things, however well the
press-work of our books might be executed, the in-
elegant appearance of the types destroyed all hope
of rivalling the beautiful productions of the European presses.

Having been long and extensively engaged in the
printing business, and suffering from the evil which
we have stated, we undertook in 1814 to establish a
new foundry, with an expectation of producing better types than were then in use; an undertaking so
difficult to accomplish, that the design must in some
degree be attributed to our want of accurate information. It was however begun and persevered in,
and is now an extensive establishment, furnishing
almost every description of types which might be
looked for in an old foundry, and some not furnished by any other. We not only produce better
types than were formerly made, but we have excited
others to improvement; and we have every reason to
be satisfied with the encouragement which we have
received in the business.[84]

Ronaldson's defense, cited in the first chapter of this
volume, denied the charges by referring to the success of the Philadelphia foundry and to the improvements of Archibald Binny. Ronaldson lashed out at
the Bruces, implying that their variations and ornaments merely increased the expense but not the
quality of printing.

Aside from stirring up animosities among former
friends, the Bruce statement testified to the change
in their attitude toward their business. Once, at the
beginning, they had intended to provide type for

[84] *A Specimen of Printing Types* (New York, 1820),
p. 1. Copy in NNC-Typ.

stereotyping; later they were fired by their ambition to possess "an extensive establishment, furnishing almost every description of types." In 1816, still the owners of a large printing plant, they had sold their printing materials to Mahlon Day and Daniel Fanshaw who became well-known printers.[85] With George Bruce managing typefounding and David Bruce stereotyping, they had set up their foundry in Hester Street.[86] Again unremitting toil paid off; in 1818 they were in a new building in Chamber Street.[87] But overwork brought ill health and retirement to David in 1822. Subsequent recovery set him going again on typefounding experiments in New York about 1826, but he soon had to resign himself to his New Jersey farm and gossip with the neighbors.[88] On a visit to his son in Brooklyn, he died on March 15, 1857.[89]

After his brother's departure from the firm George divested himself of the stereotyping business in order to spend the remainder of his life in typefounding.[90] In 1824 he issued the first of a series of specimen books (Plates 31–33). To him the love of the craft was an end in itself and through its per-

[85] "The Late George Bruce," *Typographic Advertiser*, XII (1866), 317; "Mr. George Bruce," *Typ. Mess.*, I (Sept. 1866), 81.

[86] "The Late George Bruce," *Typ. Ad.*, XII, 317; McKay, *Register*, p. 14.

[87] "The Late George Bruce," *Typ. Ad.*, XII, 317.

[88] *Longworth's New-York Directory* (New York, 1826), p. 184; "Mr. David Bruce," *Typ. Mess.*, II (March 1867), 34.

[89] *Am. Dict. Print.*, p. 73.

[90] "The Late George Bruce," *Typ. Ad.*, XII, 317.

Quousque tandem abutere, Catilina, patientia nostra? quamdiu nos etiam furor iste tuus eludet? quem ad finem sese effrenata jactabit audacia? nihilne te nocturnum præsidium palatii, nihil urbis vigiliæ, nihil timor populi, nihil consensus bonorum omnium, nihil hic munitissimus habendi senatus locus, nihil horum ora vultusque moverunt? patere tua consilia non sentis? constrictam jam omnium horum conscientia teneri conjurationem tuam non vides? quid proxima, quid superiore nocte egeris, ubi fueris, quos convocaveris, quid consilii ceperis, quem nostrum ignorare arbitraris? O tempora, o mores! Senatus hoc intelligit, consul videt: hic tamen vivit. Vivit? imo vero etiam in senatum venit: fit publici consilii particeps: notat et designat oculis

ABCDEFGHIJKLMNOPQRSTUVWXYZÆ

ABCDEFGHIJKLMNOPQRSTUVWXYZÆŒ

1234567890

Quousque tandem abutere, Catilina, patientia nostra? quamdiu nos etiam furor iste tuus eludet? quem ad finem sese effrenata jactabit audacia? nihilne te nocturnum præsidium palatii, nihil urbis vigiliæ, nihil timor populi, nihil consensus bonorum omnium, nihil hic munitissimus habendi senatus locus, nihil horum ora vultusque moverunt? patere tua consilia non sentis? constrictam jam omnium horum conscientia teneri conjurationem tuam non vides? quid proxima, quid superiore nocte egeris, ubi fueris, quos convocaveris, quid consilii ceperis, quem nostrum ignorare arbitraris? O tempora, o mores! Senatus hoc intelligit, consul videt: hic tamen vivit. Vivit? imo vero etiam in senatum venit: fit publici consilii particeps: notat et designat oculis ad cædem unumquem-

ABCDEFGHIJKLMNOPQRSTUVWXYZÆ

D. & G. BRUCE, Letter-founders,
No. 27 William-street, New-York.   JULY, 1815.

Plate 27

Quousque tandem abutere, Catilina, patientia nostra? quamdiu nos etiam furor iste tuus eludet? quem ad finem sese effrenata jactabit audacia? nihilne te nocturnum præsidium palatii, nihil urbis vigiliæ, nihil timor populi, nihil consensus bonorum omnium, nihil hic munitissimus, habendi senatus locus, nihil horum ora vultusque moverunt? patere tua consilia non sentis? constrictam jam omnium horum conscientia teneri conjurationem tuam non vides? quid proxima, quid superiore nocte egeris, ubi fueris, quos convocaveris, quid consilii ceperis, quem nostrum ignorare arbitraris? O tempora, o mores! Senatus hoc intelligit, consul videt: hic tamen vivit. Vivit? imo vero etiam in sena-

ABCDEFGHIJKLMNOPQRSTUVWXYZÆ
ABCDEFGHIJKLMNOPQRSTUVWXYZÆŒ
£ 1234567890 $

Quousque tandem abutere, Catilina, patientia nostra? quamdiu nos etiam furor iste tuus eludet? quem ad finem sese effrenata jactabit audacia? nihilne te nocturnum præsidium palatii, nihil urbis vigiliæ, nihil timor populi, nihil consensus bonorum omnium, nihil hic munitissimus habendi senatus locus, nihil horum ora vultusque moverunt? patere tua consilia non sentis? constrictam jam omnium horum conscientia teneri conjurationem tuam non vides? quid proxima, quid superiore nocte egeris, ubi fueris, quos convocaveris, quid consilii ceperis, quem nostrum ignorare arbitraris? O tempora, o mores! Senatus hoc intelligit, consul videt: hic tamen vivit. Vivit? imo vero etiam in senatum venit: fit publici consilii particeps: notat et designat oculis ad cædem unumquem-

ABCDEFGHIJKLMNOPQRSTUVWXYZÆ

D. & G. Bruce, New-York, 1816.

Plate 28

fection he saw the way to elevate the art of printing. During 1822, for example, he made the first American attempt to establish correct proportions between the proximate bodies of type. According to De Vinne:

His object was to make all types properly correlated with as little disturbance as possible to the bodies then in regular use.

As the most used bodies of brevier, long-primer, and pica were, in most foundries, very nearly correct in their relations to each other, these bodies were taken as the ones which should be least disturbed, and to which the others should be made to conform; but the intermediate and so-called irregular sizes were adjusted to the regular sizes without regard to old usage. Bruce began his change by determining the exact size of the six standard bodies from pica to minion. This done, the dimensions of larger or smaller bodies were determined by the multiplication or division of the six standard bodies. Conformity was obtained by making the bodies increase by the rule of geometrical progression. Small-pica was made as much larger than long-primer as bourgeois was made larger than brevier. Each body was made a certain percentage larger than its proximate smaller body. . . . It is ingenious and scientific, but has not been adopted by any other American typefoundry. For sizes larger than canon it is not so well adapted. All American and English founders, as well as all the manufacturers of wood types, make their larger bodies multiples of pica. Printers prefer this system for large types, not for its superior facility of combination, but for its nicer division of sizes. For the smaller types the rule of geometrical progression brings bodies too near together.[91]

[91] De Vinne, *Pract. of Typ.*, pp. 147–49.

The American Dictionary of Printing and Bookmaking supplements this description:

To complete his plan it was necessary to add agate, between pearl and nonpareil, and double brevier, otherwise known as Columbian, between English and great primer. His theory has not been adopted by other foundries to any extent. The two foundries which were older than his had nearly the same unit in pica, Bruce differing, and he also differed in sizes in which the others agreed. Job printers felt compelled to buy fonts which would match with their existing quadrats and spaces. Neither did Bruce push his sales as his competitors did theirs. It cannot be doubted, however, that his plan was the most philosophic of all.[92]

No longer concerned with time or money, he himself cut the punches and fitted up the matrices for new styles of type, borders, and ornaments. In the 1830s his Scripts found great favor; apparently he made a specialty of them, for the last set of punches he cut, when in his seventy-eighth year, was for a great primer Script.[93] The absence of self-interest in this creative talent was praised by C. C. Savage:

He was never so happy as when he could leave the details of business, and sit quietly at the bench in his private office, devising and cutting something new in typographic art. But his close application must not be attributed to considerations of economy. For no man spent money more freely, if satisfied that any improvement in the art would be developed thereby. It was his recreation. Idleness was no lux-

[92] *Am. Dict. Print.*, p. 521.
[93] "The Late George Bruce," *Typ. Ad.*, XII, 317.

Quousque tandem abutere, Catilina, patientia nostra? quamdiu nos etiam furor iste tuus eludet? quem ad finem sese effrenata jactabit audacia? nihilne te nocturnum præsidium palatii, nihil urbis vigiliæ, nihil timor populi, nihil consensus bonorum omnium, nihil hic munitissimus habendi senatus locus, nihil horum ora vultusque moverunt? patere tua consilia non sentis? constrictam jam omnium horum conscientia teneri conjurationem tuam non vides? quid proxima, quid superiore nocte egeris,

ABCDEFGHIJKLMNOPQRSTUVWXYZÆ

ABCDEFGHIJKLMNOPQRSTUVWXYZÆŒ

No. 2.

Quousque tandem abutere, Catilina, patientia nostra? quamdiu nos etiam furor iste tuus eludet? quem ad finem sese effrenata jactabit audacia? nihilne te nocturnum præsidium palatii, nihil urbis vigiliæ, nihil timor populi, nihil consensus bonorum omnium, nihil hic munitissimus habendi senatus locus, nihil horum ora vultusque moverunt? patere tua consilia non sentis? constrictam jam omnium horum conscientia teneri conjurationem tuam non vides? quid proxima, quid superiore nocte egeris, ubi fueris, quos convocaveris

ABCDEFGHIJKLMNOPQRSTUVWXYZÆŒ

£   1234567890   §

Quousque tandem abutere, Catilina, patientia nostra? quamdiu nos etiam furor iste tuus eludet? quem ad finem sese effrenata jactabit audacia? nihilne te nocturnum præsidium palatii, nihil urbis vigiliæ, nihil timor populi, nihil consensus bonorum omnium, nihil hic munitissimus habendi senatus locus, nihil horum ora vultusque moverunt? patere tua consilia non sentis? constrictam jam omnium horum conscientia teneri conjurationem tuam non vides? quid proxima, quid superiore nocte egeris ubi fueris quos

ABCDEFGHIJKLMNOPQRSTUVWXYZÆ

D. & G. Bruce, New-York, 1818.

Plate 29

ENGLISH BLACK.

We hold these truths to be self=evi=
dent: that all Men are created equal;
that they are endowed by their Creator
with certain unalienable rights; that
among these are life, liberty, and the
pursuit of Happiness; that to secure
these rights governments are institut=
A B C D E F G H I J K L M N O P
Q R S T U V W X Y Z &

PICA BLACK.

We hold these truths to be self=evident:
that all Men are created equal; that they
are endowed by their Creator with cer=
tain unalienable rights; that among
these are life, liberty, and the pursuit
of happiness: that to secure these rights
governments are instituted among men,
deriving their just powers from the con=
A B C D E F G H I J K L M N O P Q
R S T U V W X Y Z &

SMALL PICA BLACK.

We hold these truths to be self=evident: that all
Men are created equal; that they are endowed by
their Creator with certain unalienable rights; that
among these are life, liberty, and the pursuit of
happiness: that to secure these rights, governments
are instituted among men, deriving their just pow=
ers from the consent of the governed; that when=
ever any form of government becomes destructive
of these ends, it is the right of the people to alter or
A B C D E F G H I J K L M N O P Q R S
T U V W X Y Z &

D. & G. BRUCE, New-York, 1821.

Plate 30

ury to him. To bring out something new and useful was his ambition. For this he would devise and labor with unwearied perseverance, and would reject without a murmur that which had cost him months of patient toil, if it did not please his fastidious taste.[94]

George Bruce died in New York on July 5, 1866.[95] The firm which the Bruce brothers founded became part of the American Type Founders Company in 1892.

This record of American typefounders during the first quarter of the nineteenth century concludes with William Hagar who was born in Rutland, Vermont, in 1798 and served an apprenticeship to a watchmaker. At eighteen he left his home town for New York with the hope of making his way in the watch business, but found no more than irregular employment. Upon hearing that Elihu White needed help, young Hagar came to his office for an interview and his eagerness influenced White to hire him immediately regardless of his inexperience. Hagar soon earned a series of promotions which led, in a few years, to an interest in the White firm. But as he longed to be in command of his own shop, this was not enough. About 1824 Hagar purchased George B. Lothian's interest in Lothian & Pell. Pell, who was not a practical typefounder, permitted Hagar to manage the firm of Hagar & Pell, sometimes called William Hagar & Co., until its disso-

[94] Quoted in "The Late George Bruce," *Typ. Ad.*, XII, 317.
[95] *Am. Dict. Print.*, p. 73.

lution in 1830. By the time he died on December 26,
1863, William Hagar had built a distinguished career as a typefounder as well as a world-wide reputation in the industry as the owner of the Bruce Type
Casting Machine.[96]

Hagar owes his importance to his attempt to in-
troduce the "Light" face. In 1825 the firm of Hagar
& Pell offered several sizes, said to be designed and
cut by David Bruce, but printers chose instead the
"bolder faces of the time."[97] One year afterward,
the Boston Type and Stereotype Foundry advertised that it had "lately completed a series of new
Founts, cut from the latest Scotch letter, much approved for its elegance and durability."[98] But it was
not until James Conner reintroduced the "Scotch"
faces that they earned wide acceptance in the United
States. According to an anonymous historian, Conner bought Hagar & Pell's punches.[99] In 1868, however, David Bruce, Jr., discoursing on the reasons
for this change in style, said that Conner hired his
own letter-cutter:

In respect to style and fashion of American type,
we find, by reference to ancient and modern specimens, that the American article has always compared favorably with that of Great Britain, from
whence we take our models. But we find that even

[96] "Mr. William Hagar," *Typographic Messenger*, II
(May 1867), 49–50.
[97] "Mr. William Hagar," *Typ. Mess.*, II (May 1867),
49.
[98] *Boston Directory* (Boston, 1826), p. xv.
[99] "Mr. William Hagar," *Typ. Mess.*, II (May 1867),
49.

Quousque tandem abutere, Catilina, patientia nostra? quamdiu nos etiam furor iste tuus eludet? quem ad finem sese effrenata jactabit audacia? nihilne te nocturnum præsidium palatii, nihil urbis vigiliæ, nihil timor populi, nihil consensus bonorum omnium, nihil hic munitissimus habendi senatus locus, nihil horum ora vultusque moverunt? patere tua consilia non sentis? constrictam jam omnium horum conscientia teneri conjurationem tuam non vides? quid proxima, quid superiore nocte egeris, ubi fueris, quos convocaveris, quid consilii

ABCDEFGHIJKLMNOPQRSTUVWX

ABCDEFGHIJKLMNOPQRSTUVWXYZ

$ 1234567890 £

Quousque tandem abutere, Catilina, patientia nostra? quamdiu nos etiam furor iste tuus eludet? quem ad finem sese effrenata jactabit audacia? nihilne te nocturnum præsidium palatii, nihil urbis vigiliæ, nihil timor populi, nihil consensus bonorum omnium, nihil hic munitissimus habendi senatus locus, nihil horum ora vultusque moverunt? patere tua consilia non sentis? constrictam jam omnium horum conscientia teneri conjurationem tuam non vides? quid proxima, quid superiore nocte egeris, ubi fueris, quos convocaveris, quid consilii

ABCDEFGHIJLKMNOPQRSTUV

WXYZÆŒ&

GEORGE BRUCE,   NEW-YORK, 1824·

Plate 31

Quousque tandem abutere, Catilina, patientia nostra? quamdiu nos etiam furor iste tuus eludet? quem ad finem sese effrenata jactabit audacia? nihilne te nocturnum præsidium palatii, nihil urbis vigiliæ, nihil timor populi, nihil consensus bonorum omnium, nihil hic munitissimus habendi senatus locus, nihil horum ora vultusque moverunt? patere tua consilia non sentis? constrictam jam omnium horum conscientia teneri conjurationem tuam non vides? quid proxima, quid superiore nocte egeris, ubi fueris, quos convocaveris, quid consilii ceperis, quem nostrum ignora-

ABCDEFGHIJKLMNOPQRSTUVWX

ABCDEFGHIJKLMNOPQRSTUVWXYZÆŒ

$ 1 2 3 4 5 6 7 8 9 0 £

Quousque tandem abutere, Catilina, patientia nostra? quamdiu nos etiam furor iste tuus eludet? quem ad finem sese effrenata jactabit audacia? nihilne te nocturnum præsidium palatii, nihil urbis vigiliæ, nihil timor populi, nihil consensus bonorum omnium, nihil hic munitissimus habendi senatus locus, nihil horum ora vultusque moverunt? patere tua consilia non sentis? constrictam jam omnium horum conscientia teneri conjurationem tuam non vides? quid proxima, quid superiore nocte egeris, ubi fueris, quos convo-

ABCDEFGHIJKLMNOPQRSTUV

WXYZÆŒ

GEORGE BRUCE,   NEW-YORK, 1824.

Plate 32

in these grave symbols of thought and knowledge,
the capriciousness of fashion has more to do than
one would at first suspect. Much has been said of
the "Scotch face," the "turned, or filled in corner,"
as adding beauty, grace and durability to the type;
and now that the eye has become familiarized with
its appearance, we begin to think, as in the matter
of ladies' "crinoline," that there really is grace, ease
and utility in the change, however startling it may
at first have been to our staid fogyism. Hogarth's
"lines of beauty" have been quoted in support of the
change, and "square corners" pronounced as decidedly offensive to the eye.

We have before us specimen books of some of
the old British type-founders, dating as far back as
1805. In one of these they were congratulating
themselves and the public on having surmounted
some of the gross *vulgarisms* of former specimens,
among which was the "turned corner." We remem-
ber with what pleasure we gloated in admiration
over these specimens—some from the foundries of
Messrs. Caslon and Messrs. Fry & Steel, of London,
and thought they had arrived in some of their faces
to the highest point of classic proportion and artistic
finish. We have since compared these specimens,
which so much entranced our youthful mind, with
the more modern "turned corner," and, admitting
equal beauty in execution, are inclined to ascribe
any absolute improvement in appearance rather to
the love of change and the whimsicalities of fashion.

The main secret seems to be that the great improvement in printing—the ability to take a better
and more truthful impression of the face—compelled
type-founders to remodel the cut of their letter to
conform to this improvement. It is evident that the
present stubbed cut and prolonged length of hair-
line of our modern type, would be quite as unsuit-

able for "pelt balls, a Ramage press, and weak ink,"
as the best ancient type would be if worked on a
modern press. In the former case it would be an un-
sightly, continuous, black, incongruous mass, while
in the latter it would have the appearance of worn
out type, minus its hair-lines, and altogether "cur-
tailed of its fair proportions."

.   .   .   .   .

Mr. James Conner, about the year 1828, desiring
to add greater facilities to his business of stereotyping, which had greatly increased, determined to
cast his own type; but through the natural opposition of the other founders, he found great difficulty
in procuring the necessary materials. But there is
no keeping down a man of determination. Securing
to himself the services of a letter cutter, he soon gave
a new impulse to type-founding, in presenting to the
admiration of printers generally, in a well arranged
and beautifully printed miniature sheet, his series of
light face type.[100]

And so, as the first quarter of the century ended,
the demand had been met: American printers could
readily buy American type. This was reported to
the Senate in a petition of the Philadelphia book
trade, January 26, 1820: "There are five type foundries in the United States, capable of producing types
to almost any extent."[101] The founders had the ability to reach the remotest territories or the most
sparsely populated towns—wherever there was a
printing office—by their system of agents. In 1820,
for instance, James D. Bemis of Canandaigua was

---

[100] Bruce, *Typ. Mess.*, III (January 1868), 17–18.
[101] *American State Papers*, Finance, III, 463.

ABCDEFGHIJKLMNOPQRSTUVWXYZ,,;:-'.1234567890

TWO LINES NONPAREIL.

ABCDEFGHIJKLMNOPQRSTUVWXYZ,,;:.£ 1234567890 $

TWO LINES PEARL.

ABCDEFGHIJKLMNOPQRSTUVWXYZ1234567890$,,;:-'.

PICA ANTIQUE.

ABCDEFGHIJKLMNOPQRSTUVWXYZÆŒ$1234567890-,

LONG PRIMER ANTIQUE.

ABCDEFGHIJKLMNOPQRSTUVWXYZ$ÆŒ&1234567890,,;:-'.

BREVIER ANTIQUE.

ABCDEFGHIJKLMNOPQRSTUVWXYZÆŒ&$1234567890,,;:..'!?

GEORGE BRUCE,

NEW-YORK, 1824.

Plate 33

the western New York representative for both Ronaldson and Bruce.[102] Who can say what events were moulded by American founders of Boston, New York, or Philadelphia as they dispatched type to a printer opening a newspaper office in a pioneer village or a printer publishing a first reader in a town opening its first school? The drama was small in scale but epic in its influence.

The comparatively few foundries, of course, employed an increasingly greater number of men, women, and children. Although statistics of the proportions of these groups are difficult to find, one clue appears in the "Digest of Manufactures" (1823) in which the Boston typefounding industry is listed as employing seven men, two women, and four children. For Philadelphia the enumeration is twelve men and eight children.[103] This introduction of women and children in sizable numbers probably occurred between 1815 and 1820. If this is true, it would account for the decline in the number of men listed by Harry B. Weiss as typefounders in the New York directories:

1815	12
1816	12
1817	11
1818	6
1819	7
1820	9[104]

[102] Hamilton, *Country Printer*, p. 13.
[103] *American State Papers*, Finance, IV, 115.
[104] Harry B. Weiss, "Type Founders, Copperplate Printers, Stereotypers in Early New York City," *Bull. N.Y.P.L.*, LV (1951), 473.

Statistics for Philadelphia typefounders, also com-
piled by Weiss, show fluctuation, too.[105] By 1825,
then, some American typefoundries had become
enterprises of considerable magnitude, employing
a variety of personnel and successfully competing
with the import trade.

[105] Harry B. Weiss, "The Growth of the Graphic Arts in
Philadelphia, 1663–1820," *Bull. N.Y.P.L.*, LVI (1952),
140–41.

The process of making type in the beginning of the nineteenth century did not differ in any essential from type manufacture in the fifteenth century. Sometimes called the "hand-mold and spoon" method, it utilized an easily closed and separated two-part mold (Plate 34). The caster put the matrix in the bottom of the mold, then, with his right hand, he used a small ladle to pour the molten metal into the mold. With his left hand the caster shook the mold to force the metal into the crannies. Updike, noting that some letters required different motions, referred to an account of an English foundry in which "mention is made of the uncouth movements and swaying figures of a group of gray-haired type-casters, who appeared as if demented to any one who did not know what they were about."[1] After being shaken, the mold was opened and the type thrown out. The extra portion of metal on the type, the jet, was broken off by hand. Then the two broad sides of the type were rubbed on a grindstone. Following this, the type was given to the dresser who scraped the other two sides and cut the groove. Skillful casters could work rapidly. Moxon (1683) said that one man could cast four thousand letters a day; in 1750 a contributor to the *Universal Magazine* estimated production at three thousand letters a day.[2]

In America as in Europe the substitution of the machine to ease man's drudgery was changing ancient methods. Devices were being invented to improve and speed up all processes of manufacture. The account of the fourth United States patent, granted to Francis Bailey on January 29, 1791, dealing with "Punches for types, &c. &c.," is a mysterious period piece, fascinating in itself, but it also has historical overtones.[3] As one of the oldest American patents in existence, it bears a constellation of signatures: Washington, Jefferson, and Randolph, as President, Secretary of State, and Attorney-General; in the bargain Alexander Hamilton, as Secretary of the Treasury, was called upon to estimate its value. Only remnants of the description of Bailey's punches have survived, but it is possible

[1] Updike, *Printing Types*, I, 8.
[2] Updike, *Printing Types*, I, 9; A. B., "The Art of Cutting, Casting, and Preparing of Letter for Printing," *Univ. Mag.*, VI (1750), 278.
[3] *A List of Patents* (Washington, D.C., 1872), p. 4.

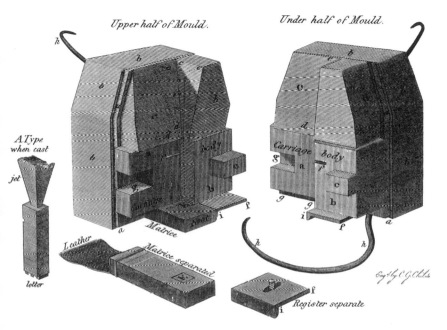

a The carriage.	b b b The wood, on which
b The body.	the bottom plate lies.
c The male guage.	c c c The mouth.
d e The Mouth-piece.	d d The throat.
f i The register.	e d d The pallet.
g The female guage.	f The nick.
h The hag.	g g The stool.
a a a a The bottom plate.	h h The spring or bow.

Plate 34 – An Engraving of a Type Mold from Abraham
Rees, *Cyclopaedia* (Philadelphia, 1810–42)

to obtain a rough idea of the purpose of his patent by following Bailey's efforts to secure it.

Even before the "Act to Promote the Progress of Useful Arts" was approved on April 10, 1790, Bailey applied for exclusive rights. On February 2, 1790, the following petition was presented to the Senate:

To the honorable the President and the honorable the Members of the Senate, of the United States of America, the Memorial and Petition of Francis Bailey of the City of Philadelphia, Printer,

Most respectfully sheweth,

That your petitioner, has invented a mode of forming Types, for printing devices, to surround, or make parts of printed papers, for any use, which cannot be counterfeited, by the most ingenious Artists in sculpture, or by any other means. That the simplicity of his invention is such, that it would be difficult to describe it, without conveying, in a very few words, the whole secret, so plainly, as to enable any artist to profit himself by the discovery. Your petitioner apprehends, that the only mode of securing to himself and his heirs, any benefit by his invention, is to disclose it, to a Committee of your honorable house, or to such heads of executive departments, as your honorable house, shall think proper to recommend, in order to obtain an exclusive right, to the use of his discovery; not doubting, but the utility of his invention, will point out the propriety of employing the petitioner, to print all such Official Papers, as may be necessary for the several Officers, within the United States, which your petitioner will undertake to execute, at the prices which you have already paid, without charging anything, for adding these inimitable devices.

Your petitioner, respectfully prays, that your honorable house, would direct an enquiry, into the

said invention, which your petitioner is ready to dis-
close; and thereupon, to encourage your petitioner,
in such manner, as his discovery shall appear to
merit.
Your respectful petitioner,
Francis Bailey.
New-York,
February 2, 1790.[4]

The Senate referred the petition to a committee
of three members who promptly fell into a quandary
about what to do next. They spent almost three
weeks thinking about the request, and on February
22 they reported back, whereupon the Senate referred the petition to the Secretary of the Treasury.[5]
Having no established rules to follow in such a case,
the committee could not make a decision and therefore retreated into the safety of silence pending the
advice of the Secretary. On the following day this
letter was read in the Senate:

Treasury Department
February 23d 1790
Pursuant to the Order of the Senate of the United
States of the 22nd of February instant, referring the
Petition of Francis Bailey to The Secretary of the
Treasury
The said Secretary
Most respectfully reports
That he has received from the said Francis Bai-

[4] National Archives, U.S. Senate (Record Group 46).
Information about this group of manuscripts was kindly
supplied by Lyle J. Holverstott in a letter of March 21,
1961.
[5] *The Debates and Proceedings in the Congress of the
United States* (Washington, 1834), I, col. 985.

ley, a communication of the Invention to which he alludes in his petition.

That it appears to him difficult to decide, to what extent that Invention will afford the Security against Counterfeiting, which is the Object of it.

That nevertheless he is of opinion, it will be likely to add to the difficulty of that pernicious practice, in a sufficient degree, to merit the countenance of Government, by securing to the Petitioner an exclusive right to the use of his Invention.

That with regard to the employment of the Petitioner to print such papers of a public nature, as may require precautions against Counterfeit; this, in the Judgment of the Secretary, ought to remain a matter of discretion, to be regulated by the success of the experiment and the convenience of the Public.

All which is humbly submitted

Alexander Hamilton
Secretary of the Treasury[6]

Hamilton, too, fought shy of a decision despite Bailey's plea that the invention was a simple one. Unfortunately Bailey's letter to Hamilton cannot be found in the National Archives, probably because Bailey, to maintain secrecy, managed to retrieve it.[7]

Bailey, at an impasse in the Senate, turned to the House for help. There his approach was more direct: on March 1 the bill "to vest in Francis Bailey the exclusive privilege of making, using, and vending to others, punches for stamping the matrices of types, and impressing marks on plates, or any other substance, to prevent counterfeits, upon a

[6] Nat. Archives, U.S. Sen. (Rec. Group 46).
[7] Information in a letter from Lyle J. Holverstott, March 21, 1961.

principle by him invented, for a term of years, was read the second time, and ordered to be engrossed."[8] On the following day it was read the third time and passed.

The text of the bill is a little more specific. In it Bailey declared that, "He hath invented a method, of making Punches for stamping and punching the matrices, of printing Types, for Letters and Devices, and for impressing on Copper, Cuts, or other printing Plates, and on Dies, & on precious metals, and on any other substances, certain marks, which Letters, Devices, and marks, cannot be counterfieted."[9] The bill gave Bailey exclusive rights to this process for fourteen years and provided for a forfeit of one thousand dollars for every infringement. It also contained a secrecy clause:

And be it farther enacted, by the authority aforesaid, that the said Francis Bailey, his Executors, Administrators or Assigns, shall within one Calendar month next, after the passing of this Act file in the Office of the Secretary of State a full, and perfect definition & specification of the Principles, of his said invention, whereby, not only, the same may be distinguished from other modes, heretofore used by others, but also, whereby an Artist, after the expiration of the said Term, may be enabled to make and use the same, *which specification shall be kept secret, and no copies thereof be delivered out, except to the said Francis Bailey, his Executors, Administrators or Assigns, until the expiration of the said Term, or until one or more actions, shall be brought by him or them, for any penalty or forfieture under*

[8] *Debates and Proc.,* II, col. 1427.
[9] Nat. Archives, U.S. Sen. (Rec. Group 46).

this Act, in which case, the Defendant or Defendants, shall be entitled to demand and receive, from the said office, a certified copy of the said specification, in order to be given in evidence, upon the Tryal, if it shall be necessary.[10]

During the legislative history of the bill several amendments were proposed. One amendment extended the filing time for the specifications from one month to six "that F B may have time to solicit his Business abroad before filing the Specification"; another proposed amendment eliminated the secrecy clause.[11] When the bill reached its second reading in the Senate, it was referred to a committee.[12] On March 4 the committee reported that "consideration thereof be postponed until a 'bill to promote the progress of useful arts' shall be taken into consideration."[13] On March 16 the bill was referred to the committee studying the bill on promoting the progress of useful arts—the general patent bill. This committee reported that the general bill would not safeguard the secret:

Francis Baileys Invention is however of such a Nature that a short & general Definition of it would expose the Secret to the Eyes of all Europe where he hopes to obtain some Reward for his Ingenuity & is taking Steps for this Purpose—his Application to the Legislature was for a special Act of Congress granting him the exclusive Privilege &c. and for Employment—he disclosed his Secret to a Committee of each House; they saw the Propriety of encouraging him & referred his Petition to the Secre-

---

[10] *Ibid.*   [11] *Ibid.*
[12] *Debates and Proc.*, I, col. 987.   [13] *Ibid.*, col. 988.

tary of the Treasury—he has reported that he
deserves Legislative Countenance by a grant of the
Exclusive Privilege but that they employing him
must be discretionary in the Departments—His Case
being particular—his Secret of great Simplicity such
as may be taken from a very slight Hint—the Prob-
ability that it will be soon known across the Atlantic
if he is obliged to advertize it as the Bill requires
—the smallness of the Reward he will be entitled to
unless by being employd as a Printer which is uncertain & precarious in its Duration, & a Variety of
other Considerations induce him to hope that a
Special Act may be passed in his Favor in which
Provision may be made that his specification filed in
the Office may not be copied by any Person until
after the End of his Term or until Actions brought
by him for Penalties render it absolutely necessary
to Defendants.

The Legislature seem in some sort bound to
grant him a special Act—had they at first said, we
are about passing a general Law which will serve
you as well as others, he would have been at Liberty
to have retained his Secret, but both Houses having
appointed Committees to whom he has disclosed it
in full Confidence of that Part of his Petition being
granted which prays for a Special Act, he seems in
some degree entitled to that Favor from Congress.

Another & very forcible Reason why a Special
Act should be granted in this Case is that it is not
a new Combination of Principles known before,
which can be exactly defined & distinguished from
all others, but it is the Discovery of a new Principle
capable of infinite Varieties in the Combination Of
Art with Accident, all of which cannot be described;
the Grant therefore would be imperfect by a Patent
—It was on this Ground that the British Parliament

pass'd an Act in 1786 securing to Bolton & Watt a new Invention to condense Steam for working Steam Engines, the Principle of which was to draw the Steam out of the Cylinder by an exhausted Receiver, which could be done in so many different Forms that had they taken a Patent for their Form, others might be used not described in their Specification & they be robb'd of the Principle of their Invention, which was therefore granted by a Special Act of Parliament—nor is there any Danger of the Precedent involving Congress in repeated Applications; for the mode adopted by the Bill for promoting Arts is so just, simple & easy to be pursued that no Inventor will undertake the Trouble of soliciting a Special Act where "the general Act" will serve him & if once in several Years a new Principle (as in the present Case) is discoverd, Congress will not find it often repeated nor too troublesome considering that such new Principle does honor to the Country, adds to the Stock of useful Knowledge & effectually promotes the Progress of the Arts.[14]

On receiving this report, the Senate voted to accept it "as amendments to" the general patent bill.[15]

After passage of the general bill and its approval, Bailey applied for his patent. On January 29, 1791, the government granted it for "certain Methods, not before known or used, for forming Punches, by which to impress on the . . . Matrices of printing Types, whether such Types be for Letters or Devices, as well as to impress on any Metal or other Substance capable of receiving and retaining Im-

[14] Nat. Archives, U.S. Sen. (Rec. Group 46).
[15] *Debates and Proc.*, I, col. 995.

pressions various Marks which are difficult to be counterfeited"[16] (Plate 35). (The ellipsis appears in the document.)

Aided by the disastrous Patent Office fire in 1836, Bailey seems to have everlastingly concealed the secret of his method for the prevention of counterfeiting. Nevertheless it is evident that his patent had no connection with punches for ordinary type.

What the typography looked like is the puzzling question. Certainly the composition was affected by the process, but was it bizarre or conventional? Neither the American Numismatic Society nor the Smithsonian Institution possesses any money printed by Bailey at that time, but a hint of the design is located in, of all places, the diary of George Washington.[17] On January 25, 1790, he recorded that Francis Bailey, "introduced by Messrs. Scott and Hartley, of Pennsylvania, and Mr. White, of Virginia, offered a paper, in the nature of a Petition, setting forth a valuable discovery he had made of marginal figures for notes, certificates, &c. which could not by the ingenuity of man be counterfeited."[18] Presumably these figures are what the Senate committee cryptically termed a "Combination of *Art with Accident.*" Did this mean a code

[16] Facsimile in U.S. Patent Office. Ervin H. Pollack informs me that the original is on display at the Ohio State University College of Law.

[17] Information in communications from George C. Miles, American Numismatic Society, March 6, 1962, and V. Clain-Stefanelli, Smithsonian Institution, March 13, 1962.

[18] William S. Baker, "Washington after the Revolution, 1784–1799," *Penn. Mag. Hist. Biog.*, XX (1896), 44.

Plate 35 – The First American Typefounding Patent

that only Bailey could unscramble? Or did it mean
some sort of random distribution? At present the
answer is not known.

Other inventors followed Bailey in devising improvements for specialized use or particular operations, but added the factors of greater quantity and
more speed. The idea of the manipulation of time
by mechanization was spreading, and a few men
were attempting to save man-hours by creating a
typecasting machine. One, Dr. Apollos Kinsley
(1766–1803), known in the history of printing for
his early model of a cylinder press, seems never to
have practiced medicine.[19] Instead he devoted much
of his life to a series of inventions for making prod-
ucts cheaply and saving time: these included, in
addition to the press, a brickmaking machine, a
horseless carriage or "steam locomotive," a machine
for cutting tobacco, a machine for casting bullets,
and a machine for currying leather. In "A Description of various Machines and Engines invented by
Mr. Apollos Kinsley, now resident in the City of
New-York," his typecasting machine is discussed:

1. For Making Printers' Types.

This machine is constructed on five different
models. The mode of operation is, by passing type-
moulds (of a new and peculiar form) under the
bottom of a vertical tube, filled with type metal, kept
constantly in a state of fusion. Forty moulds and
matrices, for different letters, are fixed in a sliding
brass frame, to move under the bottom of the tube,

[19] Biographical information about Kinsley is in Newton
C. Brainard, "Apollos Kinsley," *Bull. Conn. Hist. Soc.*,
XXVI (1961), 12–20.

containing the melted metal, and pass, in close contact, with a polished plate at the bottom of the same, by which means the moulds are filled, and the superfluous metal, or *sprews*, is cut off. The moulds are moved backward and forward under the tube, by turning a crank, and, by the same operation, the moulds open, discharge the types, and close again in continual succession.

The Encyclopaedia states, that, in the usual way, one man will cast three thousand types in a day, and another day is required to cut off the sprews. The inventor supposes that his machine will cast 5000 types in one hour, and cut off the *sprews* at the same time.[20]

Additional information about this machine cannot be found; apparently Kinsley was still working on it at the time of his death two years later.

Curiously enough, Kinsley lived in Hartford, Connecticut, between 1795 and 1798 where, at that time, Elihu White and William Wing were already intensively working on their own typecasting machine. With tolerance it may be presumed that Kinsley was unaware of this, but there is no proof either way. In the small community of Hartford, men of similar mechanical bent would, one might think, hear news of each other's activities. But the fact remains that the first two typecasting machines in the United States were designed simultaneously at Hartford. Whether this was through sheer coincidence or not, remains to be determined.

[20] "A Description of Various Machines and Engines Invented by Mr. Apollos Kinsley," *Am. Rev. and Lit. Jour.*, I (1801), 127.

On August 28, 1805, William Wing of Hartford secured a United States patent for a machine for casting types.[21] Unfortunately, as with all our early patents, the original specifications are not available although another record does exist. About the time that this patent was being issued, Elihu White, Wing's partner in the project, went to England in order to obtain British protection for the invention. He was successful, and the British patent records, therefore, contain a complete description of the machine. White was granted Letters Patent on October 23, 1806, for No. 2979, "A Machine for Casting or Founding Types, Letters, Spaces, and Quadrats, usually made Use of in Printing." The specification was acknowledged on December 19, 1806, and enrolled on April 22, 1807. It is a long and complicated specification, accompanied by a drawing (Plate 36), but an abridgment, printed by order of the Commissioners of Patents, summarizes the document:

A "slider plate," fitted with "male" and "female" sliders, moves upon "sliding ways" in a square brass frame, which extend nearly up to a "head-block" at (one end of the frame). The depth of the sliders is precisely equal to the length of the body of the letter to be cast, and the thickness of the male slider precisely equal to its size. On the slider plate being moved (by the action of a screw) towards the head-block, studs in the male sliders come in contact with the front half of a "regulating bar," which prevents their reaching the head-block, whereas the female sliders, having no studs, are driven home against

[21] *List of Patents*, p. 54.

the head-block, by which means certain spaces are left open along the head-block for the body of the letter. On reversing the screw the whole is drawn back until the studs meet the after half of the regulating bar, by which they are stopped, while the female sliders will still move back until the letters are quite clear of the sliders, so as to fall or be taken out. When letters are to be cast, a bar containing a matrix box is pressed up to the under part of the head-block and sliders, and brings the matrixes exactly under the spaces kept open by the sliders for the body of the letters, and ready to receive the metal, which is poured in through apertures in the matrix bar.[22]

Clearly this technique differed from that of Kinsley's; White and Wing attempted to cast simultaneously while Kinsley's invention cast in succession. It is worthy of note that in these first two typecasting machines invented in the United States, one embodied a typecasting principle similar to that of the Linotype and the other to that of the Monotype. These men, at one time living in the same city, approached the same problem with entirely different ideas. That neither was successful might be attributed to the difficulty of producing, at the turn of the century, a machine sufficiently precise. This, at least, was the opinion of David Bruce, Jr., himself the inventor of a well-known typecasting machine:

The impression that would almost invariably strike a thoughtful visitor on beholding for the first time the process of type-casting by the old hand-

---

[22] *Patents for Inventions* (London, 1859), XIII, 114–15.

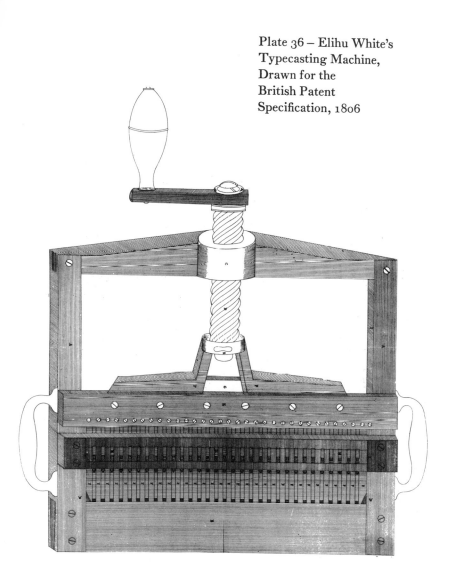

Plate 36 – Elihu White's
Typecasting Machine,
Drawn for the
British Patent
Specification, 1806

mold system, would be the apparent waste of time and labor in producing such an insignificant result—the casting of a single type! it requiring at all times great and continuous labor over a pot of molten metal. Hence, all projectors of improvement were apt to be caught in the snare of multiplying the number of types at one cast, and from their ignorance of the peculiar accuracy required, sought to give expedition by increasing the number of molds to be filled by the same operation.[23]

And so, to quote Bruce again, "from the year 1806 to 1825, no material change or attempt at improvement took place in the method of casting—the founders expending their energies in a quiet rivalry, and in increasing their business facilities on the settled old plan; turning a deaf ear to all suggestions of even ordinary advancement."[24]

Of the minor improvements patented during this period, Archibald Binny's seem to be the most significant. Again, because of the lack of official specifications, one must depend upon indirect evidence. Binny received three patents: on January 29, 1811, for an improved printers' type mold; on February 4, 1811, for a method of "smoothing or rubbing printers' types"; and on May 17, 1814, for molds for casting printing types.[25] In his evaluation of these inventions James Ronaldson may have been prejudiced when, in the 1822 specimen book, he referred to the "great improvement and much simplification" which Binny made and which reduced the business

[23] Bruce, *Typ. Mess.*, III (Nov. 1867), 1.
[24] *Ibid.*, p. 2.   [25] *List of Patents*, pp. 93, 139.

to "the reach of ordinary talents."[26] But others have
also paid tribute to Binny's type mold. De Vinne,
in doing so, described it: "In 1811, Archibald Binny
of Philadelphia devised the first improvement in
hand-casting. He attached a spring lever to the
mould, giving it a quick return movement, which
enabled the type-caster to double the old production."[27] MacKellar, too, was impressed by its effi-
ciency: "Binny made an important improvement in
the type-mould, by which a caster could cast 6000
letters in a day with as much ease as he before could
cast 4000."[28] Ringwalt added a sentence about
Binny's other invention: "By a modification of the
ancient mould, which he patented in 1811, Mr.
Binny greatly increased rapidity of production, and
at the same time rendered the labors of the caster
less arduous. He subsequently made energetic but
fruitless efforts to invent a machine for rubbing
type."[29]

The fact that Binny's patents were obtained in
1811 and 1814 suggests that he may have been inspired to work on these inventions after he had
studied the tools acquired with Franklin's equipment. A bit of evidence pointing to this appears in
Bruce's statement that Binny "acknowledged that
they received many valuable suggestions from these
tools; thereby conclusively proving that the typefounding art, as it existed at that period, was at a

[26] *Specimen of Printing Type*, p. 2.
[27] De Vinne, *Pract. of Typ.*, p. 26n.
[28] MacKellar, *American Printer*, p. 20.
[29] *American Encyclopaedia of Printing*, ed. J. Luther
Ringwalt (Philadelphia, 1871), p. 61.

much higher state of perfection in France than in Scotland or the United States."[30] Commenting on this, De Vinne said:

With this testimony as to the value of the tools, added to our knowledge of Franklin's interest in scientific instruments of every kind, it may be assumed that Fournier sold not old but new tools, and that he had provided everything needed to establish his point system in America, in the equipment which he furnished to Bache. There can be no doubt that Binny & Ronaldson had, and made use of, the Fournier mould for pica, and that the standard they fixed for this body was accepted by their successors.[31]

Others also secured patents relating to typefounding. In 1816 George Webster of New York received one for a casting device, and George B. Lothian obtained one for a type mold.[32] In 1820 George Bruce patented a method of making shaded letters.[33] All of these, apparently, were unimportant to the trade. The next major advance began when, on October 31, 1827, John Sturdevant and Edwin Starr patented their typecasting machine.[34]

While these inventions concerned metal type, it must not be forgotten that some wood type, whether domestic or imported, was occasionally used. References to it are rare and usually appear in inventories. For example, in the dissolution of the printing office

[30] Bruce *Typ. Mess.*, III (Nov. 1867), 1.
[31] De Vinne, *Pract. of Typ.*, p. 155n.
[32] *List of Patents*, pp. 164, 170.   [33] *Ibid.*, p. 214.
[34] Information in a communication from T. B. Morrow, U.S. Patent Office, March 12, 1954.

of John Hayes and Jacob A. Killen, Baltimore,
April 3, 1784, the inventory included "a captl. case
of large wooden letter some metal," and the inventory of the estate of Simon Gardner, Boston, June
12, 1824, included "3 Alphabets wooden letter."[35]
Mass-produced wood type, however, did not begin
to appear until 1828.[36]

[35] Minick, *A History*, p. 77; Rollo G. Silver, "Abstracts
from the Wills and Estates of Boston Printers, 1800–
1825," *SB*, VII (1955), 217.
[36] Rob Roy Kelly, "American Wood Type," *Design
Quarterly* 56, pp. 3–4.

Until the American founders controlled the American market, domestic printers imported most of their type from the foundries of England, Scotland, France, and Holland. Even though the familiar names of Caslon, Fry, and Wilson predominate in the annals of American printing of the period, there is evidence of other founders. It will eventually be possible to identify more of these sources by referring to the bills, account books, and advertisements of the printers as well as by the appearance of faces in extant printed material. There is also more to be learned about the importation of type in petitions relating to the imposition of tariffs.

The complicated transaction of buying abroad was bypassed by many printers who used importers as purchasing agents instead of negotiating directly with the European founders. A letter from James Rivington of New York to Isaiah Thomas, dated August 11, 1783, shows his financial policy:

The terms I deal with persons in a wholesale way is ready Cash paid in New York on delivery of my goods. I have two printing offices on the passage to me for two persons who agree to pay me 25 p Cent. advance on the Types arrival. If you desire a supply I will include the Letter you may require amongst Books &c at 12½ p Cent. ready money on their being shipped to you.[1]

Thomas later bought much type direct from England, but many printers, commonly those not near a seaport, paid the importer's commission.

In 1785 the Secretary of Congress advertised for proposals to print a new edition of the *Journals* of the Continental Congress. He received nine bids, four of which gave the origin of the types to be used. Charles Cist's specifications included the specimen of Dr. Alexander Wilson & Sons, Glasgow, 1783, as examples of his type.[2] Francis Childs, it will be remembered, stated that he expected in the next French packet a shipment from Benjamin Franklin containing "a Variety of Types—the Matrixes of which were designed by the Doctor and cast under his direction."[3] And Shepard Kollock printed his proposals and an address to Congress "with a new and elegant Type . . . cast under the immediate supervision of that great Typographer, Doctor

[1] American Antiquarian Society, Isaiah Thomas Papers. The material from the Isaiah Thomas Papers is printed by kind permission of the American Antiquarian Society.
[2] Dandridge, *SB*, II, 195.   [3] *Ibid.*

Franklin."[4] James Adams declared that he had "lately imported from London a general Assortment of Types."[5] These bids demonstrate that new type from the foundries of Scotland, France, and England was available and in use very soon after the Revolutionary War.

That same year, on the title page of *A Specimen of Isaiah Thomas's Printing Types*, the assertion (which was true) that this was as large and complete an assortment "as is to be met with in any one Printing-Office in America" was amplified by applause: "Chiefly manufactured by that great Artist, William Caslon, Esq; of London."[6] The specimen itself shows a surprisingly large collection of Caslon fonts, but that did not stop him from acquiring much additional stock: "£2,000 sterling and upwards, were added to this Specimen, in types from Fry's, Caslon's and Wilson's Foundries."[7] A bill to Thomas from Joseph Fry & Son, dated August 16, 1786, is evidence of the cost of imported type at that time:

lbs	oz			£		
480..	8	Burgs. on Brevier	2/6	£ 60..	1..	3
6..	0	Brevier flowers	2/6	..15..		
9..	8	Small Pica Do	1/2	..11..	1	
75..	0	Various Do	1/–	3..15..		
502..	8	Long Primer	1/6	37..13..	9	
	24	French Rules	6d	..12..		
		5 boxes		..8..	6	
				£103..16..	7	

[4] *Ibid.* [5] *Ibid.*
[6] Updike, *Printing Types*, II, opp. p. 157.
[7] *Ibid.*, p. 157.

Charges, viz. –
 Insurance & Policy,
   exclusive of Risq.
   of Capture   2 .. 7 .. 0
 Wharfage,
   Shipping &c   .. 2 .. 10
 Bill of Lading   .. 2 .. 6
 Primage   .. 2 .. 6   2 .. 14 .. 10
                                  £106 .. 11 .. 5[8]

Thomas's series of transactions with the Fry foundry over his well-known "Standing Bible" of 1797 were painful and frustrating to both sides, and kaleidoscopic in range. They covered seven years of delay, with money and stock tied up, and resulted in the inevitable backwash of anger and regret. In 1790 Thomas wrote to Edmund Fry & Co. to ask the cost of the type required for a nonpareil Bible and the cost of having it composed, corrected, and put in tied-up pages. The firm of Fry estimated the total at £1,444 with the provision of nine months for casting "with six good hands constantly upon it" in addition to eight or ten weeks for composition.[9] Thomas accepted the proposal, thus initiating one of the most ambitious American publishing projects of that time, a project which stirred Ebenezer T. Andrews, his partner in a Boston shop, to write: "I think you have a *type frensy*, as you term it, and that I should have one too if I had wherewith."[10] But as the years went on, it seemed as if the

[8] American Antiquarian Society, Isaiah Thomas Papers.
[9] Douglas C. McMurtrie, *The Isaiah Thomas "Standing Bible"* (Chicago, 1928), p. 9.
[10] American Antiquarian Society, Isaiah Thomas Papers, letter of E. T. Andrews, Jan. 4, 1791.

work would never be finished. Of the total of thirty-three sheets, Thomas had only received twenty by November 1794.

Thomas agonized over the delays: "It bears peculiarly hard as I have been at a great expense for Stock which must again lye dead over another winter."[11] Despite his disillusion with Fry, it must have been to his interest to continue buying from him, for he had continued to order additional equipment, including ink, presses, and more type from the foundry.[12] In turn, the firm answered soothingly on January 2, 1794, when Thomas balked at the average increase of ten per cent on the price of type:

We are a little surprised with the information thou hast sent us respecting the prices of Type quoted by Wm. Caslon—The alteration of prices were made by the full consent & under the signature of the whole Trade, as p the inclosed List, to which we refer thee —if any other prices have been sent, we beg the favor of thy noting the variation in thy next Letter, & we are determined (let the Quotations be what they may short of losing ones) not to suffer an old & good Customer to be tempted away from us.[13]

The extra business which Thomas sent must have softened their regret at having undertaken the Bible project, and perhaps at that time trade of any kind was sorely needed. Later they no longer camouflaged their true feelings. On May 21, 1796, Fry & Steele summed up a losing game: "We are very sorry, (not being Printers ourselves, & having much

[11] *Ibid.*, letter of Isaiah Thomas, Nov. 20, 1794.
[12] *Ibid.*, bill of Edmund Fry & Co., June 5, 1793.
[13] American Antiquarian Society, Isaiah Thomas Papers.

other Business to attend to,) that we undertook to have the Bible set up, whereby we have had immense trouble, & suffered great Loss and disappointment."[14]

Appraisals of imported type appear in the Thomas Papers at the American Antiquarian Society. Ebenezer T. Andrews, in his letters to Thomas from Boston, kept score on the founders, and was reluctant to order domestic type:

October 7, 1792: "I do not think Fry's ornaments equal to Caslon's—many of them are indifferent, I think."

April 28, 1793: "Larkin has received his types from Wilson."

May 12, 1793: "Peirce is going to set up at Portsmouth. His types are from Caslon's."

May 22, 1793: "Think best not get the Long Primer from Philadelphia as yours is like to come—Inclose you a letter, with a specimen of the type inclosed—it is Baine's letter, I think, and by no means handsome. Wish for your opinion respecting taking the Philadelphia type."

Another correspondent, James Grant, writing to Isaiah Thomas in August 1793, gives some reasons for the popularity of Wilson's product:

I likewise herewith send, Wilson & Co. of Glasgow's specimen of printing Types.—They are friends of mine, & one of them Doctor W. is now in town.—Their Letter for durability, as well in the face, as in the wear has very long been well known, —it has indeed of late so much established itself with the printing Trade in London, their Foundery bids fair to do twice the business of either Fry's

[14] *Ibid.*

Caslon's or Jackson's–At present the number of hands employed by them exceeds either of those long established here.–

But a very material Consideration, abstracted from superiority, is, their not having advanced their Letter with the London Type Founders,–this makes a difference in the favour of the Wilson's of 25 per Cent. & of course to all printers it forms a very material object of saving.

In Philadelphia Mathew Carey favored the domestic founders, particularly Baine and Binny & Ronaldson, whenever their product was available. But he also purchased foreign type, sometimes locally, sometimes from London. In 1787 he bought some of the small pica which Franklin brought back with him and which Franklin had originally sold to Francis Childs who returned it. The bill follows:

Mr. Carey bought of B. Franklin

```
2 Boxes of        ⎡211 lb G.
   Sm. Pica       ⎨    Weight 236
   containing     ⎣213    Do 238
Two Parcels of Sm. Pica      126
Imperfections                  1..8 oz
Do                             8..8
Do                             5..
                             ———————
                             615..0
        Deduct empty Boxes    24
                             ———————
                             591
        Sent back to be deducted  67
                             ———————
                             524 lb at 2/2 p lb
                               makes 57..  3..4
Double Rules 3 lb at 2/ p Pound makes      6..
Interlines 5 lb at 2/ p Pound makes       10..
   Do   6                                 12..
Quadts & Spaces of Double Pica
   8 lb at 2/ p lb                        16..
                                        ———————
                                        59..  7..4
```

Bought of Mr Carey 216 lb of Type
   metal at /6 p lb   5 . . 8 . .
Balance due   53 . . 19 . . 4
Deduct by an error in the 2 first articles   4
                            53 . . 15 . . 4[15]

This purchase caused much hard feeling between
Franklin and Carey. They disagreed about the
price, and Carey objected to Franklin's demand for
security of payment.[16] (The complete story of this
transaction will, of course, be recorded in Professor
Labaree's edition of the Franklin Papers.)

The delays and complications involved in importation from London agents are readily seen in the
correspondence and bills of Mathew Carey. In a
letter to Carey dated August 8, 1792, his London
agent, George Barclay & Co., acknowledged receipt
of an order:

Thro' the Channels of our Mutual & very good
friend Mr George Meade of Philadelphia we are
favored with Your's of the 25 June, Inclosing a Letter with an order for Types which we have forwarded to Dr Alexander Wilson & Sons of Glasgow & agreable to your Request have urged them to
get it ready as soon as possible & in preference if an
opportunity should offer from Greenock, to Ship it
from thence—if not to send it up here to be Ship't by
one of the New York Traders for we shall have no
opportunity Direct for Philadelphia at the time you
mention We hope however it will be nearly the same
thing to Send the Types to New York & we shall of

[15] American Antiquarian Society, Mathew Carey Papers, I, 240. The material from the Mathew Carey Papers
is printed by kind permission of the American Antiquarian
Society.
[16] Information in a communication from Leonard W.
Labaree, Oct. 26, 1962.

Course Pay for them ready Money with a Discount of 7½ pCt. as you seem to wish—[17]

Neither Carey nor Barclay realized that Wilson was fully booked. On August 25 Barclay wrote to Carey again:

The preceeding is Copy of which we had the Pleassure to write you the 8 Instant p the Ship George Barclay which we confirm we then intimated to you that we had forwarded your Letter to Dr. Alexander Wilson & Sons of Glasgow containing an Order for Types. We are sorry to inform you we have since received the answer mentioning that from their extensive Engagements it was totally impossible for them to execute it so as to be with you by the Time you limit—they therefore have declined it altogether —observing however at the same Time that they could have an excellent Fount ready for you by the first spring Ships sailing provided such an Order was handed them soon—[18]

Carey could do nothing but submit to Wilson's postponements; on February 4, 1793, Barclay wrote that "Messrs. Alexr. Wilson & Sons of Glasgow write us that they had received your Order for printing Types but as it had only lately arrived it would be utterly impossible to execute it in Time to send by the Spring Ships they however say they shall lose no Time in getting the Types ready & we have confirmed to them that we shall be answerable for the Payment of the Amount."[19]

[17] Historical Society of Pennsylvania, Mathew Carey Papers. The Barclay-Carey correspondence is printed with the kind permission of the Historical Society of Pennsylvania.

[18] Historical Society of Pennsylvania, Mathew Carey Papers.

[19] Ibid.

When Wilson did ship type, he occasionally included some for another printer. A note accompanying the first of the three following bills calls attention to this: "You will observe that one of the Bills of Loading includes a Box for Mr Thomas Dobson which Messrs. Wilson's beg you will take the Trouble of Delivery over to him."[20] These bills show the expenses of importation:

I.

Invoice of 6 Boxes Types shipped at Liverpool on board the Adriana Capn John Robertson for account & risk of Mr. Mathew Carey of Philadelphia ...

Pica fount compleat

	536 lb @ 1/	£26	16						
Two Lines do	8 8 oz 1/		8	6					
3 Boxes			6						
		£27	10	6					
Discount for ready Money 7½ pCt.		2	1	6	£25	9			
Long Primer	518 lb @ 1/6	£38	17						
two Line letter	5.8 1/		5	6					
3 Boxes			6						
		£39	8	6					
Discount for Money 7½ pCt.		3			36	8	6		
					£61	17	6		
Commission 5pCt.					3	1	10		
					£64	19	4		
Insurance on £70 @ 3 Guins pCt. £	2	4	1						
Comm. ½ pCt.	7								
Policy	7			2	18	1			
				£67	17	5			

Errors Excepted
London 3 July 1793
George Barclay & Co.[21]

[20] *Ibid.*

[21] American Antiquarian Society, Mathew Carey Papers, I, 41.

II.

Invoice of a Box Types shipped (at Liverpool) on board
the Atlantick Cap: Silas Swaine for account & risk of Mr.
Mathew Carey of Philadelphia Viz:

Brevier	206	@ 28d	£24		8				
2 Line letter	2.8	12		2	6				
Box				2					
			£24	5	2				
Discount for									
Money 7½ pCt.			1	16	2	£22	9		
Commission 5 pCt.						1	2	5	
						£23	11	5	
Insurance on £26 @ 3 Guins pCt. £				16	4				
Commn. ½ pCt.				2	7				
Policy							18	11	
						£24	10	4	

Errors Excepted
London 19th August 1793
George Barclay & Co.[22]

III.

Invoice of a Box Types shipped at Glasgow on board the
Fame Capn.—for account & risk of Mr. Mathew Carey of
Philadelphia Viz:

Pica	211 lb @ 1/–	£10	11				
Box & freight			5				
		£10	16				
Discount 7½ pCt. for Money			16	£10			
Commn. 5 pCt.					10		
				£10	10		
Insurance on £12 @ 3 Guis. pCt. £ –			7	7			
Commn. ½ pCt.			1	2			
Policy					8	9	
				£10	18	9	

Errors Excepted
London 19th August 1793
George Barclay & Co.[23]

[22] *Ibid.*, p. 42.   [23] *Ibid.*, p. 40.

In the advertisements of the 1790s and the early 1800s printers sometimes announced their recent acquisitions, usually specifying origin. The foundries were various:

April 30, 1791: Benjamin Russell, Boston, received new type manufactured in Holland.[24]

October 25, 1793: Belknap & Hall, Boston, received new type from Fry.[25]

March 21, 1794: John Hayes, Baltimore, received "an elegant and complete apparatus" from Caslon.[26]

December 9, 1797: Joseph Bumstead, Boston, received new type from Wilson.[27]

June 11, 1805: The Troy, New York, *Northern Budget* received new type from Wilson.[28]
One advertisement published by a Fry agent advises that the importer's commission would be eliminated if orders were placed through him. Evidently American business had increased to the point where, in 1794, Robert Browne of New York could offer: "The subscriber wishes to inform the Printers in the different States, that he can supply them with Printing Types of every description from Fry's celebrated Foundery, London. The Types shall be delivered in New York at cost and charges free of any commission; the money to be paid at the Current Exchange at the time of delivery."[29]

These manuscripts and advertisements, if com-

[24] *Columbian Centinel*, April 30, 1791.
[25] *Apollo*, Oct. 25, 1793.
[26] Minick, *A History*, p. 79.
[27] *Columbian Centinel*, Dec. 9, 1797.
[28] Hamilton, *Country Printer*, p. 13.
[29] New York *Herald*, Nov. 24, 1794.

prehensively searched, could be the background to an understanding of the actual appearance of the type. It is deplorable that few scholars, Morison, Conkwright, and Hyder excepted, have attempted to identify the type in American books of the period. It is hoped that these necessarily limited studies are only a beginning. At least we know that Wilson's type can be found in Aitken's 1784 edition of Blair's *Lectures* as well as in Lang's 1791 edition of *Of Commerce and Luxury* and in the final five volumes of the Bioren & Madan 1795 Shakespeare.[30] Fry's type also appears in the last two mentioned works as well as in Thompson's 1796 edition of *The Pains of Memory* and in Thompson & Small's 1798 Bible.[31] Caslon's and Bell's types were used by Colerick, Hunter & Beaumont for their almanacs for 1796 and 1797.[32] Bell type may be seen in *The Pains of Memory* and in three books published in 1800: G. & R. Waite's edition of *Desultory Reflections;* Hugh Maxwell's editions of *Pursuits of Literature* and *George Washington to the People of the United States.*[33] One more book, the Bible published at Hartford in 1809, merits attention if only to show that Thomas's experience did not discourage the intrepid Connecticut publishers. According to P. Canfield, the Bible "was set up in Nonpareil, small 12mo, making, I believe, 68 forms (34 sheets), put in chases, corrected, and shipped from the foundry

[30] Hyder, *PaGA*, IX, 70–74.   [31] *Ibid.*, pp. 73–80.
[32] Stanley Morison, *John Bell, 1745–1831* (Cambridge, 1930), p. 127.
[33] Hyder, *PaGA*, IX, 80–81; Morison, *John Bell*, p. 127.

of Wilson and Sons, Glasgow, to Hudson and Goodwin at a cost, as I have understood, of 6000 crowns."[34]

Until the list is supplemented with more such examples, it will be difficult to measure the comparative popularity of the founders. If a tabulation of who used what type can be made, it will be a prelude to judging whether the firms were favored for their low prices, easy accessibility to their product, good taste in design, or a combination of these factors. A contemporary verdict on what was aesthetically satisfactory in a type face was written by William Duane in the course of an article for the Philadelphia *Aurora* in 1802:

I will now give you a general sketch of the peculiarities of the several types of these artists. Caslon's were plain and unornamented, the small letters, that is under Great Primer, were not so destitute of beauty as those above that size. Great room was left for improvement, which in the term of 50 years were made to a considerable extent.

Baskerville's types were an improvement upon Caslon, they introduced a bolder stroke and swell of the letter, but there were many of his letters ungraceful and disproportioned. The general appearance was comparitively elegant, but much was owing to his *ink* and press-work.

Jackson had Baskervilles' bold stroke but retained the uncouth shape of his master Caslon.

Fry (or rather Moore) introduced a more beautiful shape, but the face of the letter was what printers

[34] Quoted in E. B. O'Callaghan, *A List of Editions of the Holy Scriptures* (Albany, 1861), p. 96.

call *too lean*—it was a delicate light stroke, which bore little service and soon wore down.

Wilson's of Glasgow was not quite so elegant as Moore's nor so uncouth as Jackson's—but the great merit of these types lay in their being more durable as well as handsome—the metal was uncommonly hard.

The person whom I above mentioned as superceding all these, and bringing the British press up to the highest perfection was Bulmer. The luxury of the age, and other circumstances, such as the printing for the Shakespeare Gallery in England, introduced a rage for fine printing upon vellum and hot pressing. To render typography equally worthy of regard, Bulmer adopted many improvements from engravers, and taking the bold stroke of Baskerville, adopting the swelling shape of Fry, he added thereto the delicate and brief curves of the Italians and their fine hair stroke. The types of Bulmer are now to be seen in every work of elegance or taste printed in England, and are sought after in various parts of Europe. But what is a remarkable circumstance it is necessary to wait a year before an order is executed, so great is the demand—and spare sorts are not to be had at all.[35]

This synopsis came from the experience of an American practical printer who was decidedly a connoisseur but willing to concede that durability, as in Wilson's type, was praiseworthy. He was not the only American to reconcile himself to this. William McCulloch told Archibald Binny that the castings of Justus Fox and Wilson excelled Binny's in wear and durability. Binny replied, according to McCulloch, "that they were at first so 'devilish'

[35] *Aurora*, March 2, 1802.

ugly, that the longest using cannot mar their deformity."[36] But even though a competitor thought them ugly, Wilson's sturdy type sold well in the nation.

The durability of Wilson's type was once scientifically accounted for by a group of New England printers. Sometime after its founding in 1805, the Society òf Printers of Boston and its Vicinity, also called the Faustus Association, delegated its Standing Committee to investigate the quality of available type. Joseph T. Buckingham recalled the incident:

Some of the types from the foundry of Binny & Ronaldson, of Philadelphia, had been complained of by one of the members, as of *bad quality*, and a chemist was employed by the committee to analyze the metal and determine whether it was inferior to that used in other foundries. The chemist reported that the specimens of Scotch type were by far the most durable, that the English was less so by 15 or 20 per cent., and that the American had an alloy surprisingly great. Whether the result of this investigation was transmitted to the Philadelphia founders or not, I do not recollect; but I find the record states that the difficulty in which it originated had been adjusted.[37]

Apparently French type was so seldom used that investigation was not warranted. It, too, was made of sturdy metal. McCulloch, when writing about the type inherited from his father, remembered it: "I possessed by a similar conveyance, a fount of French Brevier, which Franklin brought over from

[36] *McCulloch*, p. 168.
[37] J[oseph] T. B[uckingham], "The Faustus Association," Boston *Evening Transcript*, Sept. 7, 1859.

France, and which was used on an incredible quantity of editions of books. My father printed a great many 1000 copies of the school testament on that fount."[38]

Although Binny's type may not have been as tough as Wilson's, it had the advantage of being a domestic product, obtainable within a short time without the impediment of import laws. The tariff laws, designed to protect native industry, were considered burdensome by the printers and embraced by the typefounders. Shortly after the earliest laws went into effect, Isaiah Thomas, who was receiving type for his "Standing Bible," tried to obtain exemption from the duty of 7½ per cent ad valorem on his purchases. This duty was charged on "all other goods"; a duty on type was not specifically stated. Thomas asked General Benjamin Lincoln, Collector of the Port of Boston, to obtain a ruling from Alexander Hamilton, then Secretary of the Treasury. A draft of Lincoln's letter to Hamilton is in a Lincoln letter book recently acquired by the Massachusetts Historical Society. Under the date of September 14, 1792, he wrote to Hamilton:

My knowledge of your wishes to support the manufacturers of your Country will apologize I hope for the trouble of this Letter on the subject of tipes— Mr. Thomas of this State has it in contemplation to print the bible in two different small sizes & to do it on terms which will give him a profit . . . importing tipes sufficient for the whole work before it can be completed for they cannot do in this as in other cases set a part & break up the forms they must in order to

[38] *McCulloch*, p. 168.

save themselves set the whole & let the press stand
untill the tipes are worn out This will involve him
in an expence of about ten thousand dollars the
Duties on which is an object, he wishes to know
whether all circumstances considered they can be
dispensed with He wished to procure the tipes of
American manufactures but cannot do it.[39]

Hamilton's reply cannot be located, but Ebenezer
T. Andrews, writing on October 21, 1792, gave
Thomas a remedy:

Mr. Weld has just informed me that Gen. Lincoln
has received an answer from Mr. Hamilton to the
letter he wrote at your request respecting the duty
on types. His reply was, that had the matter been
thought of at the time of framing the bill it would
doubtless have been attended to—but that as it was
he did not know of any remedy. In consequence of
this, Mr. Weld suggested to Gen. Lincoln the idea
of having them entered as lead, as that was the chief
ingredient, and the General has consented that they
may be. Lead pays only one cent per pound wt.
which will make a very great odds in the duty, especially on the smaller types—he has also consented to
let those you last entered be done in the same way,
and if you will send down the invoice I will attend
to it—[40]

Another letter from Andrews, written eight days
later, contained less favorable news:

[39] Massachusetts Historical Society, Benjamin Lincoln
Letter Book, April 27, 1791–June 29, 1798. This draft is
printed with the kind permission of the Massachusetts Historical Society.
[40] American Antiquarian Society, Isaiah Thomas Papers.

I gave Mr. Weld your invoice but before he had time to execute the matter, Mr. Lovell suggested to Gen. Lincoln that lead was not the principal ingredient in types, but that they principally consisted of pewter—and gave it as his opinion that they could not be entered as lead, &c.—Mr. Lovell's observations so far convinced Gen. Lincoln, as to induce him to suspend the matter until he could enquire more particularly into it. Here it rests—and when you come down you must settle it as well as you can. I suppose the result will be that Gen. Lincoln will not consent to enter them as lead, without consulting Mr. Hamilton.[41]

As the duty on wares of pewter amounted to 10 per cent and the plan to enter type as lead did not appear promising, Thomas altered his tactics by sending a petition directly to Congress. On December 31, 1792, the House of Representatives received a "petition of Isaiah Thomas, of Worcester, in the State of Massachusetts, praying that printing types, of foreign manufacture, imported into the United States, may be exempted from the duty imposed on them by law; and that certain bonds, to a considerable amount, given by him to the Collector of the District of Boston, for the payment of the duties on printing types already imported, may be cancelled." The House, on the same day, referred the petition, now lost or destroyed, to the Secretary of the Treasury.[42] On February 5, 1795, he returned it to the House where, eight days later, it was re-

---

[41] *Ibid.*

[42] *Debates and Proc.*, III, col. 768; information in a letter from Harold E. Hufford, National Archives, April 17, 1961.

ferred to a committee of three members. The committee's report that "from a due regard to the advancement of the manufacture of types, and the real interests of the printing business in the United States, the prayer of the said petition ought not to be granted" was received on February 16, 1795, and "ordered to lie on the table."[43]

In the meantime, on June 7, 1794, the duty on all goods charged at 7½ per cent was raised to 10 per cent.[44] At the ports confusion about type continued with neither collectors nor printers being certain of the proper classification for these metal objects. Finally Congress resolved the matter on January 29, 1795:

Whereas difficulties have arisen in ascertaining the duties on certain articles imported into the United States, and further provisions for securing the collection of the impost duties, are found necessary:

Sec. 1. *Be it enacted by the Senate and House of Representatives of the United States of America in Congress assembled,* That in lieu of the present duties, there shall be levied, collected and paid upon all printing types which, after the last day of March next, shall be imported into the United States, in ships or vessels of the United States, at the rate of ten per cent.[45]

This tariff greatly aided Binny & Ronaldson

[43] *The Debates and Proceedings of the Congress of the United States . . . Third Congress* (Washington, D.C., 1849), cols. 1220, 1227; *American State Papers*, Finance, I, 355.
[44] *Tariff Acts Passed by the Congress of the United States from 1789 to 1909* (Washington, D.C. 1909), p. 41.
[45] *Tariff Acts*, p. 42.

when they began typefounding. As their business increased they, too, attempted to change the laws by petitioning Congress. Their petition, received on January 8, 1802, asked for a remission of duties paid on antimony and its exemption from duty. The committee of the House studying such petitions reported back with a recommendation that the duty on antimony be lifted and the duty on type be increased to 20 per cent from the prevailing 12½ per cent. As news of this spread through the book and newspaper trade, the printers and publishers held meetings in various cities and forwarded petitions of protest. The story of this printers' lobby, told in detail elsewhere, ended, as usual, in compromise.[46] Under the Tariff Act of March 27, 1804, antimony became exempt from duty, but there was no mention of any additional duty on imported printing type.

Six years later Albert Gallatin submitted his "Report on American Manufactures" in which he discussed the situation of the typefounding industry. Gallatin stated that it was firmly established, supplying at least a considerable part of the buying market. Manufacture of printing types, for which "there are two establishments, the principal at Philadelphia, and another at Baltimore, was fully adequate to the demand, but has lately been affected by the want of regulus of antimony."[47]

[46] Silver, *SB*, III, 207–28.
[47] *The Debates and Proceedings of the Congress of the United States . . . Eleventh Congress* (Washington, D.C., 1853), col. 2232.

With the industry in this rather lively condition, the War of 1812 approached and brought with it a doubling of all duties.[48] At the war's conclusion the House directed Alexander J. Dallas to submit a report on the revision of duties. This report, presented on February 13, 1816, spoke of the typefounding industry as "firmly and permanently established" and suggested that any duties should be based on national policy, the question being "between the gain of revenue and the loss of manufacture."[49] Dallas proposed the establishment of a tariff of 35 per cent on type and the admittance of antimony free of duty, but Congress laid on a duty of 20 per cent with no duty on antimony.[50] When the tariff law was reconsidered in 1820, 1823, and 1824, some members of Congress suggested an increase to 25 per cent for type, but they were unsuccessful.[51] The duty remained at 20 per cent and the American typefounding industry was sufficiently protected. It grew rapidly—but that is another story.

[48] *Tariff Acts*, p. 54.
[49] *The Debates and Proceedings of the Congress of the United States . . . Fourteenth Congress* (Washington, D.C., 1854), cols. 1683–84.
[50] *Debates and Proc. . . . Fourteenth Cong.*, cols. 1690–92.
[51] *The Debates and Proceedings of the Congress of the United States . . . Sixteenth Congress* (Washington, D.C., 1855), col. 1913; *The Debates and Proceedings of the Congress of the United States . . . Seventeenth Congress* (Washington, D.C., 1855), col. 545; *The Debates and Proceedings of the Congress of the United States . . . Eighteenth Congress* (Washington, D.C., 1856), col. 961.

INDEX

TYPEFOUNDING IN AMERICA, 1787–1825
by Rollo G. Silver
was composed by
Connecticut Printers, Inc., Hartford, Connecticut,
printed by
The Meriden Gravure Company, Meriden, Connecticut,
and bound by
Russell-Rutter Company, Inc., New York, New York.
Illustrations are by
The Meriden Gravure Company.
The paper is Mohawk Superfine.
The types are Monticello and Bulmer.
Design is by Edward Foss.